EDUCATION IN A COMPETITIVE AND GLOBALIZING WORLD

COST AND ACCESS ISSUES IN LAW AND MEDICAL SCHOOLS

EDUCATION IN A COMPETITIVE AND GLOBALIZING WORLD

Additional books in this series can be found on Nova's website under the Series tab.

Additional E-books in this series can be found on Nova's website under the E-books tab.

EDUCATION IN A COMPETITIVE AND GLOBALIZING WORLD

COST AND ACCESS ISSUES IN LAW AND MEDICAL SCHOOLS

DANIELLE B. VESSER
EDITOR

Nova Science Publishers, Inc.
New York

For permission to use material from this book please contact us:
Telephone 631-231-7269; Fax 631-231-8175
Web Site: http://www.novapublishers.com

NOTICE TO THE READER

LIBRARY OF CONGRESS CATALOGING-IN-PUBLICATION DATA

Cost and access issues in law and medical schools / Danielle B. Vesser.
p. cm.
Includes index.
ISBN 978-1-61122-529-7 (hardcover)
1. Law schools--United States--Costs. 2. Law schools--Accreditation--United States. 3. Medical education--United States. I. Vesser, Danielle B.
KF273.C64 2010
340.071'173--dc22
2010041296

Published by Nova Science Publishers, Inc. † New York

CONTENTS

PREFACE

The federal government invests significantly in medical education through various programs to help ensure that the anticipated supply of new physicians meets the nation's health care needs. Additionally, in order to participate in federal student financial aid programs, law schools must be accredited by an agency recognized by the Department of Education. Accreditation is intended to ensure that schools provide basic levels of quality in their educational programs, and Education recognizes those accrediting agencies that it concludes can reliably determine the quality of education provided by the schools and programs they accredit. This new book examines the cost and access issues facing students in law and medical schools across the United States.

Chapter 1- The federal government invests significantly in medical education through various programs to help ensure that the anticipated supply of new physicians meets the nation's health care needs. Medicare, the federal health care program for elderly and certain disabled people, subsidizes training for medical school graduates in hospitals and other teaching institutions by helping to support the increased costs associated with postgraduate medical training. These subsidy payments provided hospitals and other teaching institutions with an additional $8.76 billion[1] for postgraduate medical training in fiscal year 2008.[2] In addition, Medicaid, a joint federal and state program that finances health care for certain low-income individuals, provides funding for graduate medical education.[3] In order to pay for medical school tuition and related fees, students often rely on loans to finance their education. The Department of Education (Education) administers loan programs that are available to medical school students.[4] These loans may be made by private lenders and guaranteed by the federal government or made directly by the federal government through a student's school. The Health Resources and Services Administration (HRSA) administers various scholarships, loans, and loan repayment programs for disadvantaged students and those committing to practice in underserved areas or train in specific specialties.[5] In addition, the Department of Veterans Affairs provides funding and training

Chapter 2- In order to participate in federal student financial aid programs, law schools must be accredited by an agency recognized by the Department of Education (Education).[1] Accreditation is intended to ensure that schools provide basic levels of quality in their educational programs, and Education recognizes those accrediting agencies that it concludes can reliably determine the quality of education provided by the schools and programs they accredit. The American Bar Association's (ABA) Council of the Section of Legal Education and Admissions to the Bar serves as the main accrediting agency for law schools, and students who attend one of the 200 ABA-accredited law schools can take the bar examination in any jurisdiction in the country. There are also several law schools that are accredited by other Education-recognized accrediting agencies such as the Western Association of Schools and Colleges. Graduates of some of these non-ABA-accredited law schools are eligible to take the bar examination in their own state, but may not do so nationwide.

Chapter 3- In order to participate in certain federal programs, such as federal student financial aid, postsecondary institutions must be accredited by an accrediting agency recognized by the Department of Education (Education). Accreditation ensures that schools provide basic levels of quality in their educational programs, and Education recognizes those agencies it concludes can reliably determine the quality of education provided by the schools and programs they accredit. Since 1952, Education has recognized the American Bar Association (ABA) as an accrediting agency for law schools. ABA accreditation is important to the 195 law schools it accredits because it allows their graduates the flexibility to take the Bar exam in any jurisdiction in the United States.

In: Cost and Access Issues in Law and Medical... ISBN: 978-1-61122-529-7
Editors: Danielle B. Vesser

Chapter 1

GRADUATE MEDICATION EDUCATION: TRENDS IN TRAINING AND STUDENT DEBT

United States Government Accountability Office

May 4, 2009

The Honorable George Miller
Chairman
The Honorable Howard P. "Buck" McKeon
Ranking Member
Committee on Education and Labor
House of Representatives

The Honorable Robert Andrews
Chairman
Subcommittee on Health, Employment, Labor and Pensions
Committee on Education and Labor
House of Representatives

The Honorable Charles W. Boustany, Jr.
The Honorable Joe Courtney
The Honorable Tom Price
House of Representatives

Subject: *Graduate Medical Education: Trends in Training and Student Debt*

The federal government invests significantly in medical education through various programs to help ensure that the anticipated supply of new physicians meets the nation's health care needs. Medicare, the federal health care program for elderly and certain disabled people, subsidizes training for medical school graduates in hospitals and other teaching institutions by helping to support the increased costs associated with postgraduate medical training. These subsidy payments provided hospitals and other teaching institutions with an additional $8.76 billion[1] for postgraduate medical training in fiscal year 2008.[2] In addition, Medicaid, a joint federal and state program that finances health care for certain low-income individuals, provides funding for graduate medical education.[3] In order to pay for medical school tuition and related fees, students often rely on loans to finance their education. The Department of Education (Education) administers loan programs that are available to medical school students.[4] These loans may be made by private lenders and guaranteed by the federal government or made directly by the federal government through a student's school. The Health Resources and Services Administration (HRSA) administers various scholarships, loans, and loan repayment programs for disadvantaged students and those committing to practice in underserved areas or train in specific specialties.[5] In addition, the Department of Veterans Affairs provides funding and training opportunities for new physicians in its medical facilities.[6]

Students must complete an undergraduate education and typically 4 years of medical school, at which point they earn a medical degree and become physicians. By their last year of medical school, students typically choose a specialty in which they will undertake required postgraduate medical training, known as residency, in order to practice medicine without supervision. Most specialties can fall into three general categories: primary care, surgical, and procedural. Most students apply for residency through the National Resident Matching Program (NRMP),[7] which matches applicants with residency programs based on the preferences of both parties.[8] However, because more students apply for some specialties than positions are available, some students may not receive a position in their preferred specialty. Residency can last 3 to 5 years, depending on the specialty. After residency, some physicians may decide to pursue further postgraduate medical training, known as a fellowship, in order to become a subspecialist. For example, to become a cardiologist, a medical school graduate must complete an internal medicine residency followed by a cardiology fellowship. In some cases, depending on the specialty or subspecialty, a physician could spend 7 or more years in postgraduate medical training.

You asked us to provide information on graduate medical education. Specifically, we focused on (1) trends in postgraduate medical training, (2) factors that influence medical students' specialty choice, and (3) trends in the amounts of student debt incurred by medical school graduates. Enclosure I contains information on graduate medical education. You also asked us to provide information on trends in postgraduate dental education and student debt and thoracic surgery fellowships; that information can be found at enclosures II and III, respectively.

To examine trends in postgraduate medical training, we reviewed relevant academic and professional literature and analyzed data on residency offered, student preferences, and residency placements from 1998 to 2008.[9] We also interviewed officials and reviewed information or documents from the Centers for Medicare & Medicaid Services (CMS), the agency that oversees the Medicare program; the Medicare Payment Advisory Commission; HRSA; and professional organizations, including groups that represent medical schools, medical students, and physicians. To examine factors that influence medical students' specialty choice, we reviewed relevant academic and professional literature and examined a survey of 4th year medical students developed by the Association of American Medical Colleges (AAMC).[10] We also interviewed officials from professional organizations, including groups that represent medical schools, medical students, and physicians. To examine trends in medical student debt, we analyzed self-reported student indebtedness data from the AAMC survey of 4th year medical students from 1998 to 2008. We also examined data on medical school tuition and fees from an AAMC survey of medical schools and physician salaries collected by the Medical Group Management Association (MGMA). We also interviewed federal officials and reviewed relevant agency guidance to identify the types of federal loans and repayment plans that are available to medical students.

We discussed the NRMP, AAMC, and MGMA data sources with knowledgeable officials and determined that the data were sufficiently reliable for our purposes. (See encl. IV for a more detailed description of our scope and methodology.) We conducted our work from September 2008 to April 2009 in accordance with all sections of GAO's Quality Assurance Framework relevant to our objectives. The framework requires that we plan and perform the engagement to obtain sufficient and appropriate evidence to meet our stated objectives and discuss any limitations in our work. We believe that the information and data obtained, and the analysis conducted, provide a reasonable basis for any findings and conclusions.

In summary, we found that medical students prefer surgical and procedural specialties, and physician subspecialization is increasing. Relative to the number of available residency positions, more medical students have preferred surgical and procedural specialties over primary care specialties since 1999, according to national data. As a result, surgical and procedural specialties have been more competitive than primary care specialties. Students earning an MD degree from U.S. medical schools fill higher proportions of the more competitive surgical and procedural residency positions than students earning a DO degree and students graduating from international medical schools. In addition, the percentage of physicians pursuing subspecialty training grew from 2002 to 2007, according to national data.

This trend was observed in fields such as orthopedic surgery (a surgical subspecialty), anesthesiology (a procedural specialty), and family medicine (a primary care specialty).

Multiple factors and demographic characteristics influence students' specialty choice. While there is no consensus on the most influential factors affecting specialty choice, students consider various factors either individually or in concert when selecting a specialty, according to multiple sources, including published literature, a 2008 AAMC survey, and experts we interviewed. For example, students may consider their intellectual interest in the specialty, their exposure to the specialty, or the prestige of the specialty when making their specialty choice. Some factors may also lead students to pursue certain specialties while avoiding others. For example, the desire for a controllable lifestyle—a predictable schedule and fewer on-call hours[11]—and high salary may lead students to pursue procedural specialties such as anesthesiology, and avoid other specialties such as primary care. Demographic characteristics such as gender and marital status are associated with students being more likely to enter certain specialties. For instance, married students are more likely to select primary care specialties and women are more likely to select obstetrics and gynecology and less likely to choose surgery.

Although medical student debt is rising, physicians are eligible for federal loan repayment relief plans during postgraduate medical training and can eventually earn high incomes that can be used to repay their loans. Medical school tuition and fees have increased significantly since 1998. Medical students can borrow up to $40,500 per year through the federal Stafford loan program[12] with additional funding available through other federal loan programs; these loan programs can cover the full cost of medical school. The median amount of educational debt for indebted medical students graduating in 2008 was $155,000—a 53 percent increase since 1998, controlling for inflation. Once out of medical school, residents earn stipends—on average about $3,729 a month for a 1st year resident. With $155,000 in debt, a resident's monthly loan payment could reach over $1,700 (about 48 percent of pretax income). However, residents have repayment options that can reduce their monthly debt payment until they complete postgraduate training. One option that will be available to borrowers after July 1, 2009, would cap the average 1st year resident's loan payments at about $364 month while a second option—forbearance—allows for a temporary postponement or reduction in loan payments. Physicians generally do not qualify for these options once postgraduate training is complete because, although they incur more debt than other advanced degree holders, they also earn higher incomes.

We provided a draft of this chapter to the Deparment of Health and Human Services (HHS), the department that oversees CMS and HRSA; Education; and AAMC. HHS's written comments are reprinted in enclosure V. HHS, Education, and AAMC also provided technical comments, which we incorporated as appropriate.

HHS remarked that GAO reported an increase in the specialty choice of family medicine by U.S. medical school graduates. However, we did not state this in our report; rather, we noted that physician subspecialization was generally increasing and that this trend was observed within several specialties, including family medicine. In other words, the incidence of physicians who have already chosen family medicine as their specialty but pursue additional training beyond initial residency has increased. As we noted in our analysis of U.S. MD student preferences relative to positions available, primary care specialties, which include family medicine, have been less popular than surgical and procedural specialties.

HHS also commented that service obligation—that is, a requirement that physicians practice in a specific field of medicine under certain conditions in exchange for benefits, such as educational scholarships or loan repayment—is an additional factor that potentially influences specialty choice.[13] For example, medical students can apply to HHS's National Health Service Corps (NHSC) Scholarship Program to receive funds[14] if they agree to complete a primary care residency and practice in an underserved area after residency. The NHSC also offers a loan repayment program for primary care physicians practicing in an underserved area. In our report, we focused on broad, underlying factors that affect students' specialty choice rather than specific contractual obligations.

Providing oral comments on a draft of this chapter, the AAMC largely agreed with our findings and noted that the report captured the complexities of medical students' decision making in choosing a specialty. It also added several relevant points. First, additional demographic characteristics, such as the geographic background (e.g., urban or rural) and the socioeconomic status of the medical student and his or her family, are associated with specialty choice. It added that debt does not appear to significantly influence specialty choice, which is consistent with our findings. Second, entry rates for various specialties are influenced by numerous factors, including the prevailing market conditions and environment. As a result, it noted, trends in specialty choice often shift and have been cyclical over time. For example, primary care specialties were more popular in the mid 1990s when managed care was introduced and the anticipated demand was high. And third, there is an emerging trend of physicians who provide general medical care only in hospitals where they may often work set shifts instead of being on call. The trend, which is particularly associated with physicians specializing in internal medicine (but not subspecializing), limits the number of physicians providing primary care services in traditional settings, such as physicians' offices and health clinics.

In addition, the AAMC raised concerns about including neurology and pathology in our procedural specialties category. It suggested that we consider categorizing them as "cognitive" or "other" specialties. While we did not create another category for these specialties, when we conducted an additional analysis that removed them from the procedural specialties category in our preferences-to-positions ratio analysis, we found that their exclusion did not change the trend for procedural specialties from 1998 to 2008.

If you or your staff have questions about this chapter, please contact Kathleen M. King at (202) 512-7114 or KingK@gao.gov, or George A. Scott at (202) 512-7215 or ScottG@gao.gov. Contact points for our Offices of Congressional Relations and Public Affairs may be found on the last page of this chapter. GAO staff members who made key contributions to this chapter are listed in enclosure VI.

Kathleen M. King

Kathleen M. King
Director, Health Care

George A. Scott
Director, Education, Workforce, and
Income Security Issues

ENCLOSURE I

Graduate Medical Education: Trends in Training and Student Debt

Briefing for the Staff of:
The Honorable George Miller
Chairman
The Honorable Howard P. "Buck" McKeon
Ranking Member
Committee on Education and Labor
House of Representatives

The Honorable Robert Andrews
Chairman
Subcommittee on Health, Employment, Labor
and Pensions
Committee on Education and Labor
House of Representatives

The Honorable Charles W. Boustany, Jr.
The Honorable Joe Courtney
The Honorable Tom Price
House of Representatives

Overview

- Introduction
- Objectives
- Scope and Methodology

- Background
- Results

Introduction

- The federal government invests significantly in medical education to help ensure that the anticipated supply of new physicians meets future health care needs.
- Federal government support includes:
  - Medicare payments, which provided about $8.7 billion to hospitals and other institutions for medical training in fiscal year 2008.
  - Medicaid payments, which provided nearly $3.2 billion in 2005.
  - Student loans, tuition assistance, and student loan repayment.
  - Training opportunities at federal facilities.

The road to becoming a doctor can be long and costly

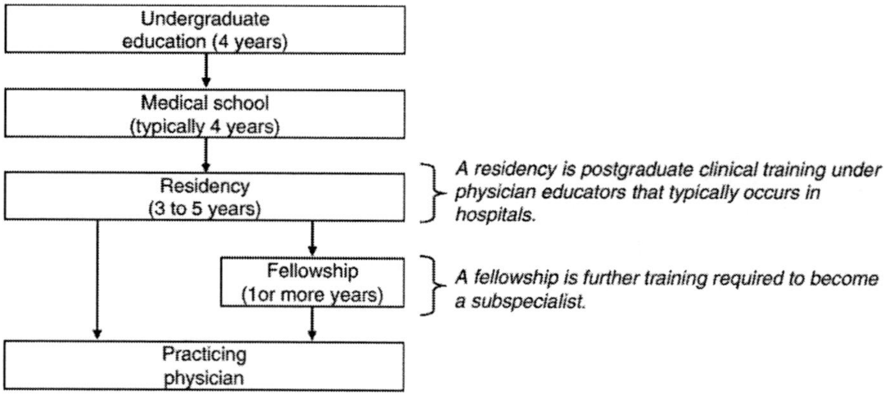

Source: GAO.

Objectives

1. Describe the trends in postgraduate medical training.
2. Describe the factors that influence medical school students' specialty choice.

3. Describe the trends in the amounts of student debt incurred by medical school graduates.

Scope and Methodology

- We reviewed relevant literature published from 1998 to 2008 from:
  - 16 research databases
  - 162 articles on residency trends, factors affecting specialty choice, and student debt
- We interviewed officials and reviewed information or documents from:
  - Centers for Medicare & Medicaid Services
  - Health Resources and Services Administration
  - Department of Education
  - Medicare Payment Advisory Commission
  - Professional organizations, including groups that represent medical schools, medical students, and physicians
- We reviewed and analyzed publicly available data, including:
  - National Resident Matching Program (NRMP) data for 1998-2008 on residency positions offered, student preferences, and placements.
    - The NRMP matches applicants with residency programs.
  - Association of American Medical Colleges (AAMC) survey of 4th year medical students, called the Graduation Questionnaire, which covers factors that may affect specialty choice. It also contains information on student debt.
  - Medical Group Management Association (MGMA) Physician Compensation and Production Survey data on median annual earnings for various medical specialties.

Background

Medical education

- U.S. medical school enrollment has grown.
  - In 2008, over 22,500 1st year students were enrolled, an all-time high.

- Eligible applicants for U.S. postgraduate medical training programs include:
  - **Doctor of Medicine (MD)** students graduating from a U.S. medical school.
  - **Doctor of Osteopathic Medicine (DO)** studentsgraduating from a U.S. osteopathic medical school.
  - **International medical school students,** who can be U.S. citizens or non-U.S. citizens graduating from a foreign medical school.
- The length of residency training varies depending on the specialty chosen.
  - Three years for primary care fields, such as family medicine, general internal medicine, and general pediatrics.
  - Five years for general surgery.
- Fellowship training to become a subspecialist can add one or more years.
  - To become a cardiothoracic surgeon, a medical school graduate must complete a general surgery residency followed by a cardiothoracic surgery fellowship.
  - To become a cardiologist, a medical school graduate must complete an internal medicine residency followed by a cardiology fellowship.

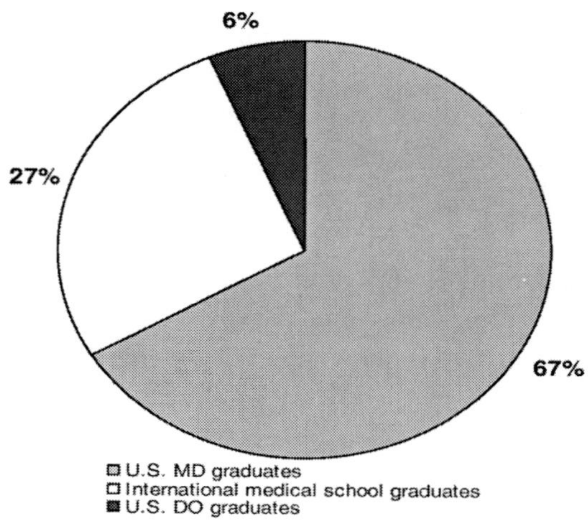

Source: AAMC and the American Medical Association (AMA)

Percentage of Physicians in Postgraduate Medical Training by School Type -2007

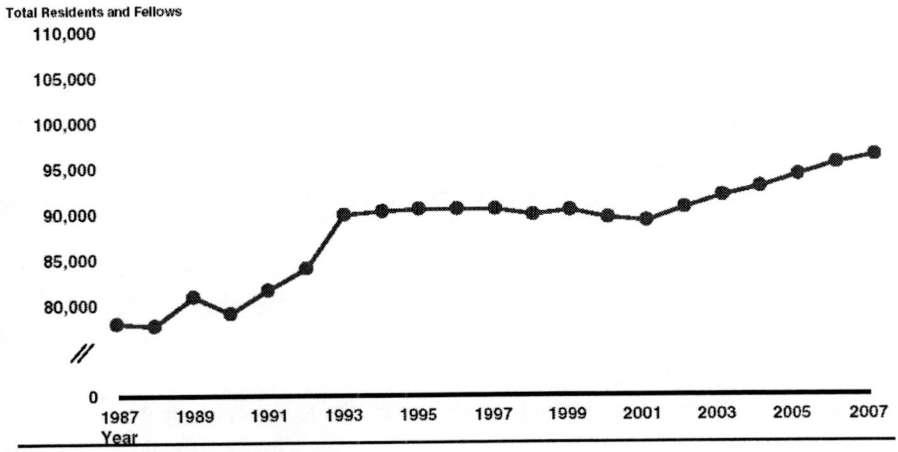

Sources: AMA and AAMC data.

Total Number of Residents and Fellows in ACGME Accredited Postgraduate Training Programs, 1987-2007

- Postgraduate medical training generally occurs at hospitals, medical centers, and Veterans Affairs facilities.
    - Each program determines how many residents or fellows it would like to train.
    - Most postgraduate training programs are accredited by the Accreditation Council for Graduate Medical Education (ACGME), which evaluates a program's ability to adequately train the desired number of residents by considering the program's facilities, faculty size, and other factors.

Key Policy Changes in Postgraduate Medical Training

- In part to constrain costs, Congress limited the number of postgraduate medical training positions supported by Medicare with the 1997 Balanced Budget Act.
- In 2003, ACGME implemented a limit on resident and fellow duty hours during postgraduate medical training due to concerns regarding residents' and fellows' work schedules and patient safety.
    - Duty hours must be limited to 80 hours per week and 1 day out of 7 days must be free from all educational and clinical obligations.

Federalstudent loans

- Loans available to students pursuing higher education:
    - Stafford Loans—the government's largest student loan program.
        - Depending on the student's financial need, these loans can be subsidized (the government pays interest while the student is in school) or unsubsidized.
    - PLUS Loans—provide more funding for graduate students who have met their maximum Stafford loan eligibility.
    - Perkins Loans—low-interest rate loans for students with exceptional financial need.
- Low-interest rate loans available to students in health professions:
    - Loans for Disadvantaged Students—for students from disadvantaged backgrounds.
    - Primary Care Loans—for students who agree to practice in primary care.

Most specialties can fall into three categories

- **Primary care specialties** include family medicine, general internal medicine, and general pediatrics.
- **Surgical specialties** include general surgery, and subspecialties in orthopedic, plastic, and thoracic surgery.
- **Procedural specialties** include radiology, dermatology, and anesthesiology, as well as subspecialties in cardiology, rheumatology, and immunology.

Summary of Findings

1. Medical students prefer surgical and procedural specialties, and are more likely to subspecialize.
2. Multiple factors and demographic characteristics influence specialty choice.
3. Although medical student debt is rising, federal loan repayment relief plans offer assistance during training and physicians can earn high incomes that can be used to repay their loans.

1: Surgical and Procedural Specialties Preferred, and Subspecialization Increasing

Surgical and Procedural Specialties Have Been More Competitive

- Since 1999—after accounting for the number of positions available—more U.S. MD students have preferred surgical and procedural specialties over primary care specialties, according to national data.
- Because more students prefer surgical and procedural specialties relative to the number of available positions, these specialties have been more competitive.
- Since 2004, surgical specialties have been the most competitive.

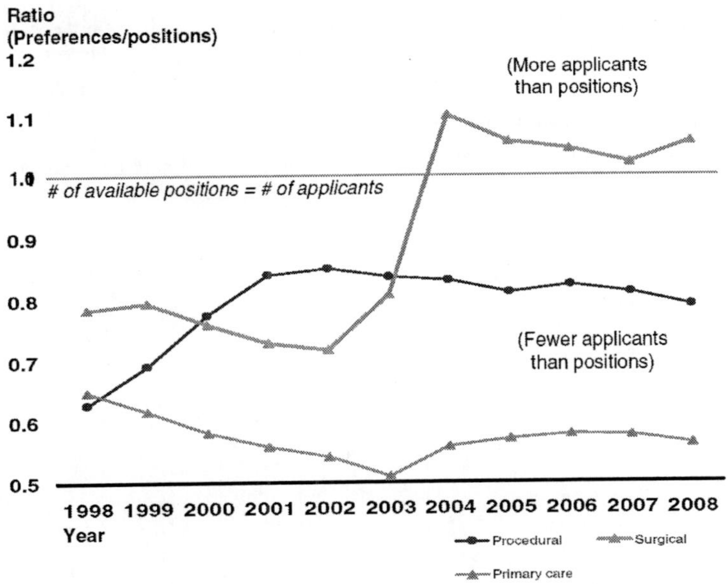

Source: GAO analysis of NRMP data.

Number of U.S. MD Student Applicants who Prefer the Specialty Group Relative to the Number of Available Positions in the Specialty Group, 1998-2008

1: Surgical and Procedural Specialties Preferred

U.S. MD students fill higher proportions of available surgical and procedural positions

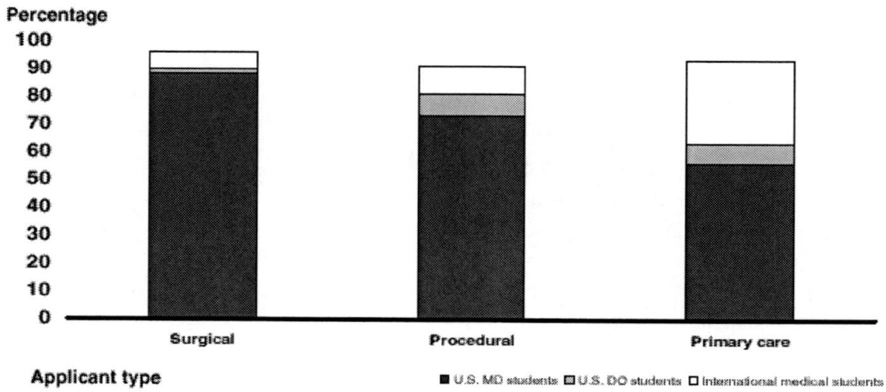

Source: GAO analysis of NRMP data.

Note: Bars do not add to 100 percent because other student groups, such as previous U.S. MD graduates and Canadian students, are not included.

NRMP Positions Filled by Applicant Type, 2008

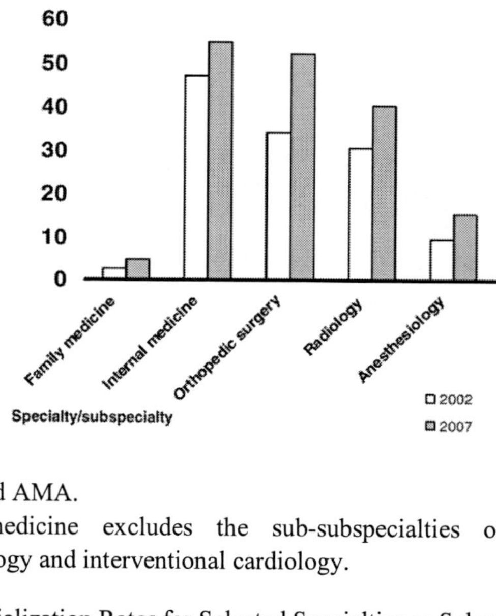

Source: AAMC and AMA.

Note: Internal medicine excludes the sub-subspecialties of clinical cardiac electrophysiology and interventional cardiology.

Change in Subspecialization Rates for Selected Specialties or Subspecialties

More doctors are pursuing training to become subspecialists

- Across selected specialties, the percentage of physicians subspecializing grew from 2002 to 2007, according to national data. This trend was also observed for family medicine.
- The majority of newly accredited programs in recent years are for training in subspecialties, according to ACGME officials. In contrast, the number of newly accredited programs for initial residency training has been relatively stable.

2: Multiple Factors, Demographic Characteristics Influence Specialty Choice

Students consider multiple factors

- Students consider multiple factors—individually or in concert—when choosing a specialty, as suggested by published literature, a 2008 AAMC survey, and experts.
  - While there is no consensus regarding the most influential factors, there are several commonly cited factors, including...

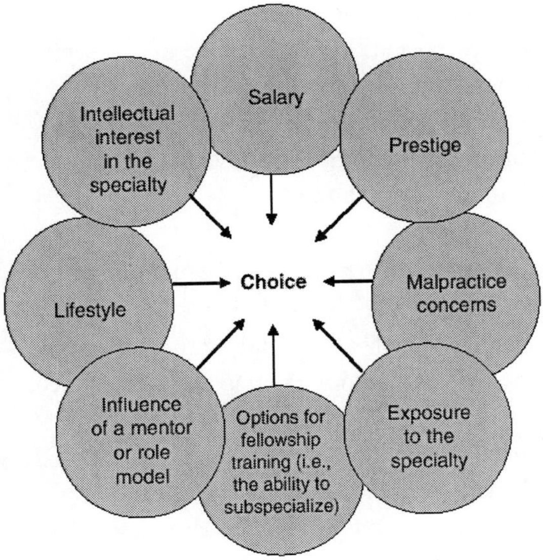

Source: GAO.

2: Multiple Factors Influence Specialty Choice

Factors lead students to pursue or avoid certain specialties

- Intellectual interest in the specialty
  - Students are attracted to rheumatology because they are interested in the complexity of diseases treated by rheumatologists.
  - Some students do not choose primary care specialties because they prefer to focus in a specialized area of medicine.
- Exposure to specialties in medical school
  - Students who had a community-based primary care experience during medical school were more likely to select a primary care specialty.
  - Students may be less likely to select surgery because they found their surgical work repetitive during medical school.
- Prestige
  - Students view surgery as prestigious while primary care specialties may not be considered as prestigious.
- Salary and lifestyle
  - Procedural specialties, with generally higher salaries and a more controllable lifestyle, may be more attractive.
    - An anesthesiologist earns about $400,000 a year, according to the MGMA, and can have a predictable schedule with fewer on-call hours.
- Primary care specialties, with generally lower salaries and a less controllable lifestyle, may be less attractive.
  - A family medicine physician earns about $174,000 a year, according to the MGMA, and can have a less predictable schedule with more on-call hours.

Demographics and personality traits are important

- Demographics—such as marital status and gender—and personality traits may be associated with specialty choice, according to published studies.
  - Married students are more likely to enter primary care specialties such as pediatrics and family practice.
  - Women are more likely to choose primary care and obstetrics and gynecology, but less likely to choose surgery.

- Personality traits, such as altruism, may lead some to select primary care specialties, while students who have competitive personalities may select surgery.

3: Debt is Rising but Federal Assistance is Available and Physicians Can Earn High Incomes

- Median debt of indebted graduating U.S. MD students has increased by 53 percent since 1998, controlling for inflation.
- The median level of debt among indebted U.S. MD students graduating in 2008 was $155,000.

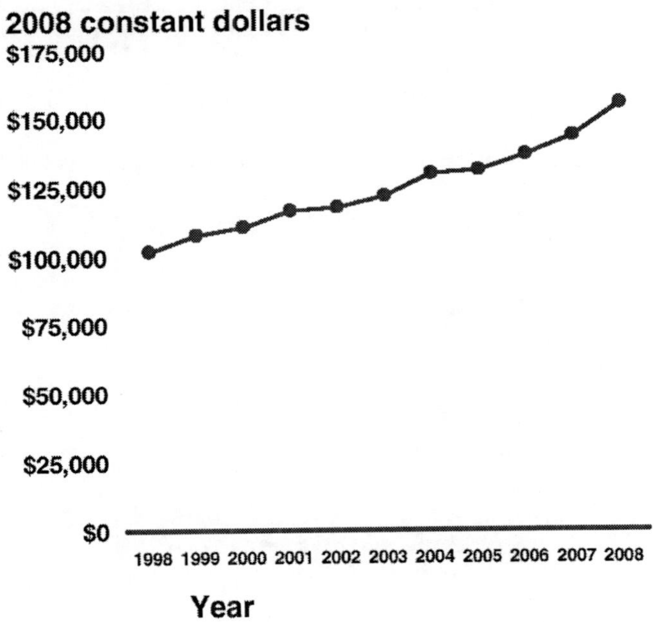

Source: AAMC.

Median Educational Debt for Indebted Graduating U.S. MD Students, 1998-2008

3: Debt, Federal Assistance, Physician Income

Nearly half of graduating medical students are at least $150,000 in debt

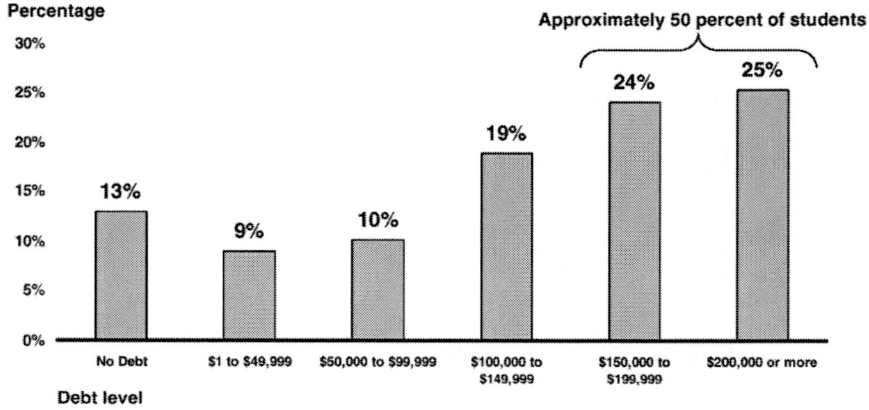

Source: AAMC.

Distribution of Student Debt Among U.S. MD Students Graduating in 2008

Medical school tuition is also increasing

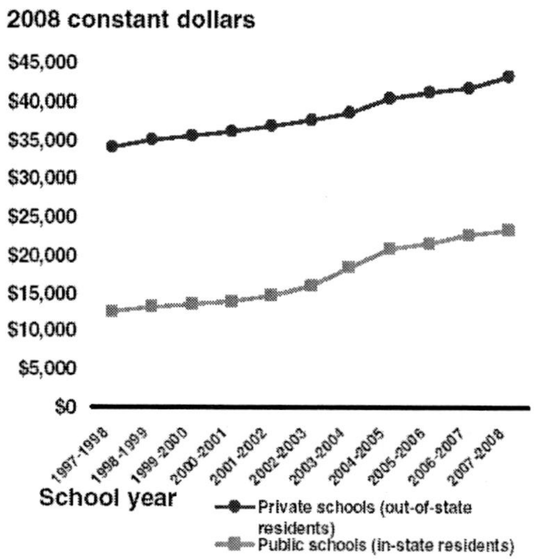

Source: AAMC.

Median Tuition and Fees for First-Year U.S. MD Students, 1998-2008

- Median tuition and fees for 1st year U.S. MD students have increased by about $9,100 at private schools (27 percent) and about $10,500 at public schools (83 percent) since the 1997-1998 school year, controlling for inflation.
    - Undergraduate tuition and fees have also increased.
- In the 2007-2008 school year, median tuition and fees for 1st year U.S. MD students ranged from approximately:
    - $23,000 at public schools (in-state residents) to
    - $43,000 at private schools (out-of-state residents)

Federal loans are available to cover the full cost of medical education

- Stafford loans—medical students can borrow up to $40,500 a year, with an aggregate limit of $224,000 (including undergraduate loans).
    - The annual limit is $20,000 more than other students can borrow.
    - The aggregate limit is $85,500 more than other students can borrow.
    - The Department of Education increased the aggregate loan limit for medical students from $189,125 to $224,000 in April 2008.

Sample Annual Budget for Student Attending Private Medical School

Cost of attendance*

Tuition and fees	$48,000
Expenses	+$19,000
Total cost	**$67,000**

Federal loans available

Stafford loan	$40,500
PLUS loan	+$26,500
Total borrowed	**$67,000**

Students can also receive financial aid from scholarships, grants, and other loan programs.

* Based on average costs reported by the five medical schools with the highest tuition and fees according to AAMC. Expenses include such costs as books, supplies, housing, food, and transportation.

Source: GAO.

- PLUS loans—graduate and professional degree students can borrow up to the full cost of attendance minus other federal assistance.

Options for reducing repayment burdens until after training

- Borrowers generally must start repaying their loans within 6 months of graduation.
    - With $155,000 in debt, a resident's monthly loan payment could reach over $1,700 per month. Since the average 1st year resident stipend is $3,729, these payments would account for about 48 percent of pretax income.
- Repayment relief options:
    - 20/220 Pathway (available until June 30, 2009)—a temporary deferment of loan payments for students with high debt relative to income.
        - Eligible residents can defer all federal loan payments without accruing interest on subsidized loans.
    - Income-based repayment plan (available after July 1, 2009)—a graduated repayment plan for students with high debt relative to income.
        - Caps the average 1st year resident's loan payments at $364 per month (about 10 percent of pretax income).
    - Forbearance—a temporary postponement or reduction in loan payments.
        - Residents are automatically eligible, but interest continues to accrue on all loans and is added to the principal. As a result, the amount due on the loans is larger than it would be if residents had not sought forbearance.
- After postgraduate training is complete, physician income typically increases significantly. At this higher income level, borrowers generallydo not qualify for repayment relief options.

Physicians incur more debt but can earn high incomes to repay it

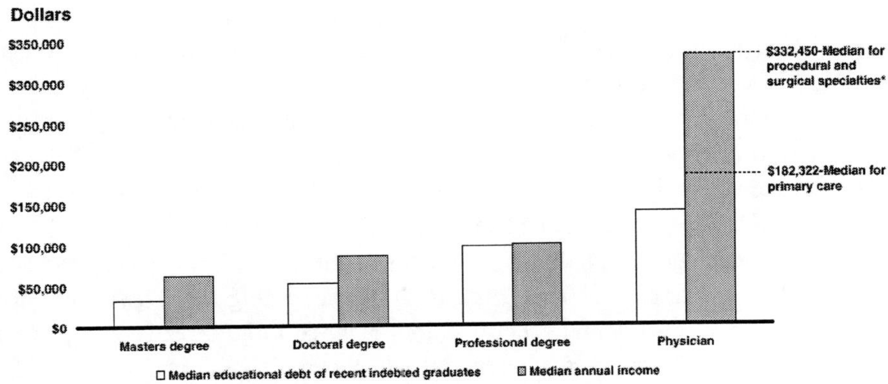

Source: GAO analysis based on data from the AAMC, MGMA, National Postsecondary Student Aid Study, and Census Bureau.

*Due to the way MGMA data is reported, the specialties included in this calculation are somewhat different from the procedural and surgical categories used in earlier slides.

Median Income and Debt by Degree, 2007

ENCLOSURE II

Trends in Postgraduate Dental Education and Student Debt

Unlike physicians, dentists are generally not required to complete postgraduate training, but may instead practice after graduating from a 4-year dental school and completion of licensure requirements, according to the American Dental Association (ADA). However, dentists may choose to pursue postgraduate training through a general or specialty dental program.

General dentistry programs last 1 or 2 years and are affiliated with dental schools, which typically offer advanced education in general dentistry (AEGD) programs, or hospitals, which typically offer general practice residency (GPR) programs. Specialty dental programs allow a dentist to train in one of several specialties—endodontics, orthodontics and dentofacial orthopedics, oral and maxillofacial surgery, oral and maxillofacial radiology, oral and maxillofacial pathology, periodontics, pediatric dentistry, prosthodontics, or public health dentistry. Many of these programs last from 1 to 3 years.[15] Some specialty programs also include graduate-level coursework leading to an additional degree.

This enclosure describes: (1) trends in postgraduate dental training, (2) factors that influence dental school graduates' choice to pursue postgraduate training, and (3) trends in debt for graduating dental students. We relied on multiple methodologies to conduct our work, including data analysis, literature review, and interviews with experts in dental education, such as the ADA and the American Dental Education Association (ADEA). (See encl. IV for a detailed description of the scope and methodology.)

The percentage of graduating students planning to pursue postgraduate dental training was stable from 1995 to 2006, according to ADEA data (see figure 1). While most dental school seniors planned to go directly into private practice, almost 40 percent planned to pursue postgraduate dental training. The rest planned to go into teaching, research, administration, government service, or were undecided.

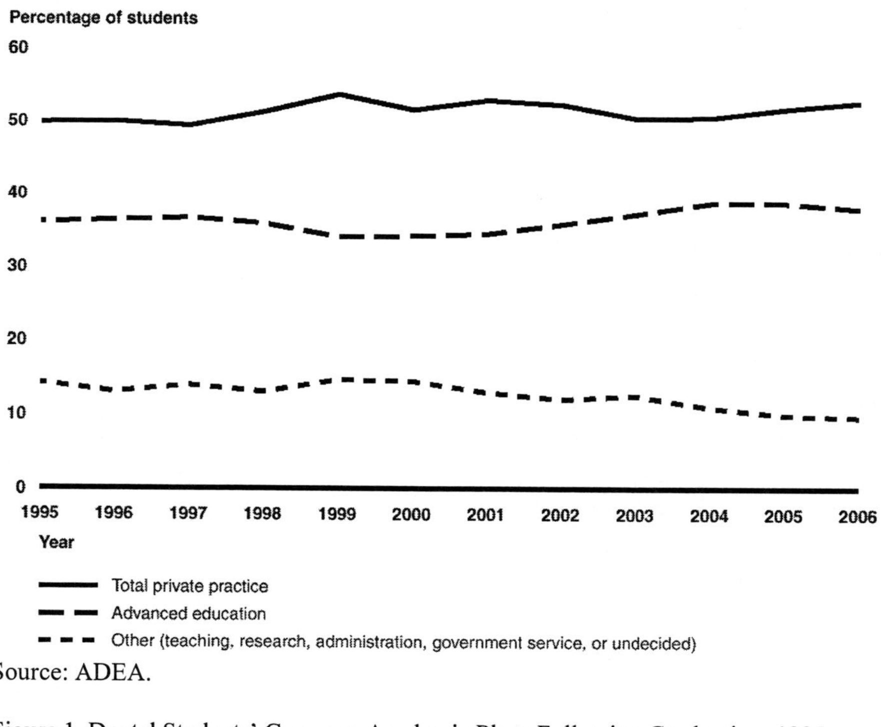

Source: ADEA.

Figure 1. Dental Students' Career or Academic Plans Following Graduation, 1995-2006

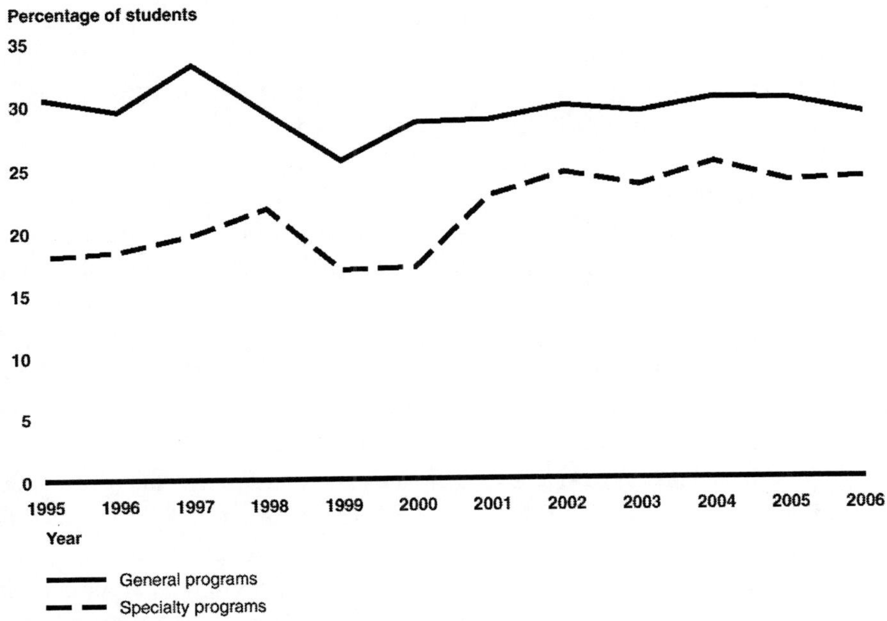

Source: ADEA.

Figure 2. Percentage of Dental Students Applying for General Programs or Specialty Programs, 1996-2006

The percentage of graduating seniors applying to general programs remained stable at about 30 percent from 1996 to 2006. The percentage of those applying to specialty programs grew from about 18 percent in 1996 to about 24 percent in 2006—over a 30 percent increase in the percentage of students applying to specialty programs over a 10- year period (see figure 2). Despite the increase in the percentage of students applying to specialty programs between 1996 and 2006, ADA data show that the proportion of specialists in the dental workforce remained close to 20 percent from 1991 through 2005. According to 2006 ADEA data, orthodontics was the most popular dental specialty (about 32 percent of specialty program applicants), followed by pediatric dentistry (about 24 percent) and oral and maxillofacial surgery (about 17 percent).

Dentists often choose to pursue postgraduate dental training because of personal interest in the content of a program, according to research studies and experts. For example, dentists may be interested in the intellectual content, diagnostic challenges, or the skills and talents required for a particular specialty. Experts also indicated that competitiveness—the applicant's ability to obtain a training position—influences whether a student applies for postgraduate dental training. Data from the 2006 ADEA survey of graduating dental school seniors show that debt influences their postgraduate plans—22 percent noted it as a major influence on their decision.

Dental student debt is rising. In 2006, the average indebtedness of all graduating dental students was $145,465—up about 55 percent from 1996, after controlling for inflation—according to ADEA data. Average tuition and fees for 1st year dental students was $29,717 for the 2006-2007 school year—up about 40 percent from the 1997-1998 school year, after controlling for inflation—according to ADA data. Average tuition and fees for the 2006-2007 school year were $17,866 for public dental schools and $41,568 for private dental schools. Average tuition and fees for the 1997-1998 school year were $8,529 for public dental schools and $25,798 for private dental schools.

Like physicians in residency, dentists can qualify for the same loan repayment relief options—income-based repayment plans and forbearance—while they are completing their postgraduate dental training.[16] In addition, like physicians, dentists can earn high incomes once their training is complete. In 2005, the average salary was $198,350 for general dentists, and $304,020 for dentists who specialized, according to the ADA.

ENCLOSURE III

Trends in Thoracic Surgery Fellowships

Thoracic surgery fellowships are an exception to the generally increasing rate of subspecialization among physicians. Forty percent fewer physicians applied for 2008 thoracic surgery fellowship positions than those applying for 2004 positions, according to national data (see figure 3). Moreover, less than 67 percent of 2008 positions were filled, down from 94 percent of 2004 positions (see figure 4). (See encl. IV for a detailed description of our scope and methodology.)]

Published articles suggest that fewer employment opportunities for thoracic surgeons may be contributing to the declining interest in thoracic surgery fellowships. For example, some thoracic surgeons may need an additional fellowship focusing on a narrower area of thoracic surgery, such as adult cardiac surgery, to secure employment. Another reason for the decline, according to experts, may be due to the growing use of nonsurgical treatments for cardiovascular disease, such as stents,[17] that are not performed by thoracic surgeons.

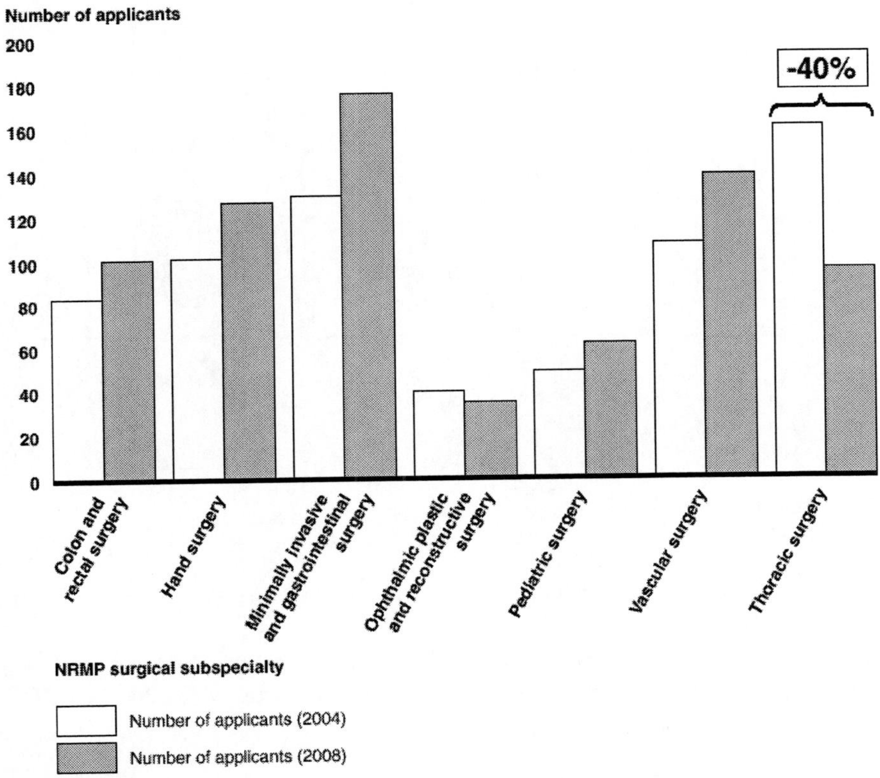

Source: NRMP.

Notes: Years refer to the year of appointment, that is, the year the physician begins his or her fellowship. Includes only surgical subspecialties for which 2004 and 2008 data were available.

Figure 3. Number of Fellowship Applicants for Selected National Resident Matching Program (NRMP) Surgical Subspecialties, 2004 and 2008

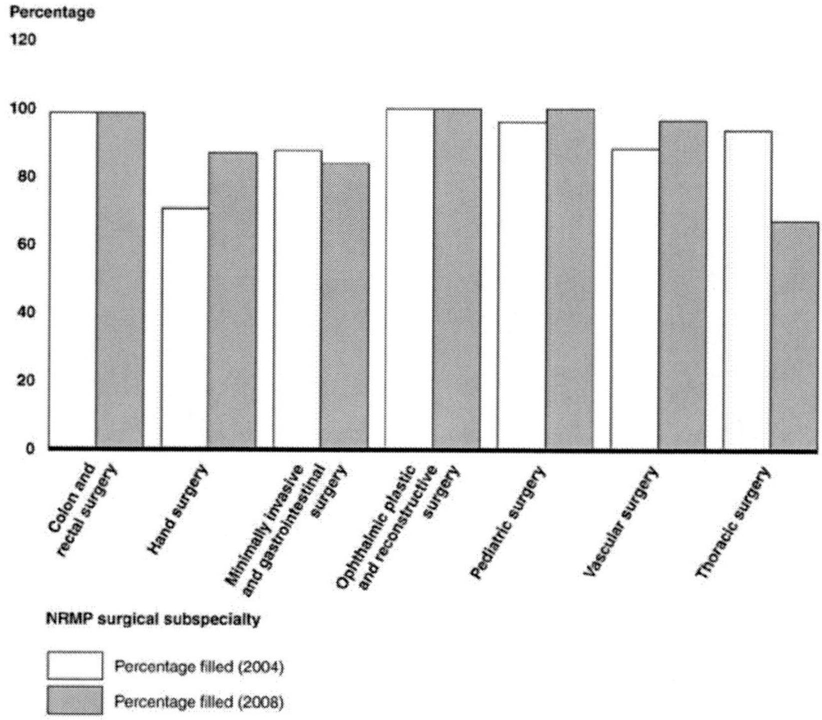

Source: NRMP.

Notes: Years refer to the year of appointment, that is, the year the physician begins his or her fellowship. Includes only surgical subspecialties for which 2004 and 2008 data were available.

Figure 4. Percentage of Fellowship Positions Filled for Selected NRMP Surgical Subspecialties, 2004 and 2008

ENCLOSURE IV

Scope and Methodology

Our review focused primarily on medical students enrolled in U.S. medical schools leading to the degree of Doctor of Medicine (MD) and allopathic[18] postgraduate medical training.[19] To conduct our work, we relied on multiple methodologies, including analyses of summary data, literature reviews, and interviews.

Data Analysis

To examine trends in postgraduate medical training, we examined National Resident Matching Program (NRMP) data for 1998 to 2008. The NRMP administers a service—known as the match—that matches applicants with residency programs based on the ranked preferences of both parties.[20] The NRMP collects and maintains data on the number of applicants, the type of applicants' medical school,[21] the applicants' preferred specialty (their first or only choice), and the specialty in which the applicant placed. According to the NRMP, the match fills about 80 percent of all residency positions. NRMP is the most comprehensive data source on student preferences and available residency positions. In addition, U.S. MD students are required to enter the match when applying for residency.[22] In 2008, 28,737 applicants applied to the match and 23,674 were successfully matched to a position. NRMP data are publicly available on the NRMP Web site.

To examine trends in U.S. MD students' preferences, we calculated a ratio of the number of U.S. MD student applicants who preferred primary care, surgical, or procedural specialties to the number of 1st and 2nd year residency positions available in each specialty group. (See table 1 for the NRMP specialties and subspecialties categorized under the primary care,[23] surgical, and procedural specialty groups; the numbers of student preference and available positions; and the ratio of student preferences to positions.) To determine the proportion of U.S. MD students, DO students, and international medical students that filled surgical, procedural, and primary care positions in 2008, we divided the number of students from each type of medical school that had received a position in primary care, surgical, or procedural specialties by the number of 1st and 2nd year positions available in each specialty group. (See table 2 for the number of students that filled each specialty category.)

To examine factors that influence specialty choice, we reviewed data from AAMC's Graduation Questionnaire (GQ). The data are available on the AAMC Web site. The GQ is an annual survey of 4th year MD students at U.S. medical schools. The survey asks students to rate the importance of factors that influence their specialty choice; students do not rank the factors in order of importance. We examined data from 2005 to 2008 because the factors listed in the survey for these years were considered to be comparable by AAMC officials. The response rate for the survey for these years ranged from 33 percent in 2005 to 71 percent in 2008.[24] Despite the variation in the response rates from 2005 to 2008, our analysis generally revealed little change in the influence of the factors on specialty choice. We therefore only reported data for 2008.

Table 1. Categories of NRMP Specialties and Subspecialties and U.S. MD Student NRMP Preferences and Positions Available in 2008

Category	NRMP specialties/ subspecialties	Number of U.S. MD student applicants who expressed the specialty category as a preferred choice (2008)	Number of positions available (2008)	Ratio, preferences to positions (2008)
Primary care	family medicine internal medicine pediatrics	5,992	10,643	0.56
Surgical	general surgery neurological surgery orthopedic surgery plastic surgery otolaryngology urology	2,217	2,093	1.06
Procedural	Anesthesiology dermatology emergency medicine neurology radiology radiation oncology pathology physical medicine and rehabilitation	4,605	5,831	0.79
Total		**12,814**	**18,567**	**N/A**

Source: GAO and GAO analysis of NRMP data.

Notes: NRMP included combined internal medicine and pediatrics programs in its preference data; however, NRMP does not consider preliminary or transitional year programs a preference for a specific specialty, and therefore they were excluded from its preference data. We grouped NRMP applicants into three specialty categories, and therefore did not include all NRMP applicants in our analysis. We also did not include specialties or subspecialties with fewer than 10 NRMP positions (with the exception of combined programs, which NRMP included under internal medicine and pediatrics accordingly). In addition, obstetrics/gynecology and psychiatry were not included because of debate within the industry about whether they are considered primary care specialties. However, including them in our preferences-to-positions ratio did not change the trend for primary care specialties from 1998 to 2008. In providing comments on our report, AAMC stated that neurology and pathology are not typically considered procedural specialties. When we conducted an additional analysis that removed them from the procedural specialties category in our preferences-to-positions ratio analysis, we found that their exclusion did not change the trend for procedural specialties from1998 to 2008.

Table 2. Number of U.S. MD, DO, and International Medical Students that Filled Each Specialty Category in 2008

Category	U.S. MD students	DO students	International medical students
Primary care	5,926	784	3,207
Surgical	1,843	34	133
Procedural	4,287	449	596
Total	12,056	1,267	3,936

Source: GAO analysis of NRMP data.

Notes: For purposes of consistency, we excluded the same programs and specialties or subspecialties as we did in our preferences-to-positions ratio analysis; we also excluded combined programs with less than 10 NRMP positions and those in which the first specialty mentioned was not included in our original definitions of primary care, surgical, and procedural.

To examine trends in student debt, we reviewed median summary data for 1998 to 2008 from the GQ published in the *AAMC Data Book: Medical Schools and Teaching Hospitals by the Numbers* (May 2008 edition), also available on the AAMC Web site.[25] The GQ asks 4th year medical students about their outstanding loans for both medical school and undergraduate education. The data are self-reported near the time of students' exit interviews with their financial aid office, when they are informed of their debt levels. The overall response rate for the survey has ranged from 33 percent to 92 percent since 1998, but this variation does not appear to have resulted in any year-to-year irregularity in the data. To validate the GQ debt data, AAMC officials compare the aggregate student-reported data with administrative records from medical school financial aid offices. The AAMC debt data are widely used because they are the most comprehensive available. Further, we also compared the AAMC data with data obtained from Education's National Postsecondary Student Aid Study (NPSAS) of 2000 and 2004. The comprehensive, nationwide NPSAS is designed to determine how students and their families pay for postsecondary education and includes data on outstanding student loan debt. We determined that average medical student debt levels from the NPSAS were comparable with the AAMC data. We adjusted the historical AAMC debt data for inflation using the gross domestic product price index. We also calculated estimated monthly loan payments for medical school graduates using the median level of student indebtedness reported by the AAMC. Our calculation was based on the assumption of a 10-year repayment schedule at the standard Stafford loan interest rate of 6.8 percent. Our calculated loan payments corresponded with estimates produced with Education's repayment plan calculator available on its Web site.[26]

To examine medical school tuition and fees, we examined data from the AAMC Tuition and Student Fees Survey of allopathic medical schools, published in the *AAMC Data Book: Medical Schools and Teaching Hospitals by the Numbers*. We adjusted the AAMC median historical data for inflation using the gross domestic product price index. To create an example of an annual medical student budget, we examined cost of attendance estimates from the five medical schools with the highest tuition and fees according to AAMC. These estimates are developed by each school's financial aid office and reflect the average estimated cost of attending medical school.

To examine the expected income of medical school graduates, we reviewed 2007 data from the Medical Group Management Association's (MGMA) *Physician Compensation and Production Survey: 2008 Report Based on 2007 Data*. The report contains the median compensation for physicians by specialty and also overall median compensation for the categories of primary care and specialists. The MGMA category of specialists includes specialties that we considered procedural or surgical specialties (for example, anesthesiology and orthopedic surgery). (See table 1.) It also includes specialties we excluded in our analysis of NRMP data (for example, obstetrics/gynecology) and additional specialties not included in the NRMP data (for example, gastroenterology). (See table 3.) However, because of the way MGMA data were reported, we were unable to recalculate median compensation amounts based solely on the specialties included in our NRMP categories . Therefore, we considered the MGMA category of specialists to correspond roughly to our combined categories of procedural and surgical.

To collect these data, the MGMA mailed surveys to 9,975 of its member organizations, which include medical group practices and other organizations involved in physician practice management. The response rate was about 20 percent. The MGMA defines compensation to include the amounts reported on W-2, 1099, or K1 (for partnerships) tax forms plus all voluntary salary reductions. The MGMA instructs respondents to include the following sources of compensation: salary, bonus and/or incentive payments, research stipends, honoraria, and distribution of profits. According to MGMA officials, they ensure the reliability of the data by examining them for inconsistencies and comparing them with other industry studies. Although multiple compensation surveys are available, we used the MGMA data because they have been used in many health policy research articles and were recommended by experts we interviewed. In addition, the Centers for Medicare & Medicaid Services uses MGMA compensation data when setting Medicare physician payment rates.

To analyze median debt and income for other advanced degree holders, we reviewed debt data from the NPSAS of 2004 and income data from the Census Bureau's 2008 Current Population Survey (2007 data), the most recent years for which data are available. To account for the different years, we adjusted the 2004 NPSAS data for inflation to 2007 dollars using the gross domestic product price index. The Current Population Survey reports median earnings for full-time workers age 25 and over by educational attainment. These sources provide data on holders of three types of advanced degrees: masters degree (including M.S., M.Ed., and M.B.A.), doctoral degree (e.g., Ph.D.), and professional degree (including M.D. and J.D.), which is required for practicing in certain professions.

To examine trends in postgraduate dental training, we reviewed publicly available data for 1995 to 2006 from the American Dental Education Association's (ADEA) Survey of Dental School Seniors. The survey asks about students' choice to pursue dentistry, educational debt, and postgraduation plans. The response rate was 84 percent in 2006 and about 79 percent from 1995 through 2006. Using the survey data, we created three categories for students' postgraduation plans: private practice, advanced education, and other. For private practice, we included students who planned to pursue solo private practice, enter a partner or group practice, or begin as an associate or employee of a private practice. For advanced education, we included students who planned to enter general practice residency or advanced education in general or specialty dental programs. For other, we included students who planned to pursue teaching, research or administrative positions, or government service, and those who are undecided. To examine trends in debt for graduating dental students, we reviewed data from the same survey. We adjusted the ADEA historical data for inflation using the gross domestic product price index. The number of U.S. dental school graduates ranged from 3,930 in 1997 to 4,515 in 2006.

To examine dental school tuition and fees, we reviewed data from the American Dental Association's (ADA) 2006-2007 Survey of Dental Education, which contains information on 1st year tuition and fees. All U.S. dental schools are required to complete the survey to maintain their accreditation status. We adjusted the ADA historical data for inflation using the gross domestic product price index.

Table 3. GAO Categories and MGMA Categories and Specialties/ Subspecialties

GAO category	MGMA category		Specialties/subspecialties
Primary care	Primary care	Family Practice Internal Medicine	Pediatrics/Adolescent Medicine
Procedural and surgical	Specialists	Anesthesiology Cardiology: Invasive Cardiology: Noninvasive Dermatology Emergency Medicine Gastroenterology Hematology/Oncology Neurology Obstetrics/ Gynecology	Ophthalmology Orthopedic Surgery Otorhinolaryngology Psychiatry Pulmonary Medicine Radiology: Diagnostic Surgery: General Urology

Source: GAO, MGMA.

To examine trends in thoracic surgery fellowships, we reviewed publicly available NRMP fellowship data on surgical subspecialties for 2004 and 2008. We included only surgical subspecialties for which 2004 and 2008 data were available.

We determined that data from the NRMP, AAMC, MGMA, ADA, and ADEA were sufficiently reliable for our purposes. We assessed the reliability of the NRMP data by interviewing NRMP officials about the residency matching process, data entry procedures, and data accuracy assurance. We assessed the reliability of the AAMC GQ data by interviewing AAMC officials about the survey methodology, response rate, and changes in the data over time. We also corroborated the GQ debt data against similar NPSAS data for selected years. We assessed the reliability of the MGMA data by interviewing MGMA officials about the survey methodology, data entry procedures, and the data accuracy assurance. We assessed the reliability of the ADA and ADEA data by reviewing documentation about the survey methodology and the response rates for the ADA Survey of Dental Education and the ADEA Survey of Dental School Seniors.

Literature and Document Review

We also reviewed literature published from 1998 to 2008 that included research articles identified through 16 databases such as MEDLINE,

PsycINFO, Social SciSearch, and Gale Group Health and Wellness. To examine trends in postgraduate medical training (including thoracic surgery fellowships), we searched "trends, medical residencies," "applications, medical residencies," "trends, physician supply," and other such terms. To examine the factors that influence medical students' specialty choice, we searched terms such as "lifestyle," "salary," "Medicare payments," "job market," and "debt." We also reviewed relevant articles from the annual medical education issue of the *Journal of the American Medical Association*. We also included in our review articles that were identified by government officials and representatives of professional associations we interviewed. We identified the factors influencing specialty choice by determining those frequently mentioned in the articles we reviewed. We then corroborated that these factors had been mentioned by experts as being influential or were identified as having influenced the specialty choice of most student respondents to the AAMC GQ survey. In all, we reviewed 162 articles.

To examine trends in postgraduate medical training and the factors affecting specialty choice, we reviewed information or documents provided to us by the Centers for Medicare & Medicaid Services, Health Resources and Services Administration (HRSA), and the Council on Graduate Medical Education. We also examined documents provided to us by the professional organizations we interviewed. (See below for the full list of government agencies and professional organizations we interviewed.)

To identify the types of federal loans and repayment plans available to medical students, we reviewed relevant regulations and guidance from Education and HRSA of the Department of Health and Human Services. We used these documents to evaluate eligibility requirements and the general terms of the loan programs.

To provide information on postgraduate dental education and the factors that influence dental specialization, we reviewed research articles that were published from 1998 to 2008. We identified research articles through 18 databases and searched using such terms as "dental residencies," "dental specialists," "salary," "lifestyle," and "training". We reviewed a total of 28 articles. The articles were used to inform our findings on postgraduate dental education and to supplement the information we obtained from experts and publicly available data from the ADA and the ADEA.

Interviews with Government Officials and Professional Groups

To gather information on medical and dental education and training, we interviewed officials from government agencies and the following professional organizations, including groups that represent medical schools, medical students, and physicians:

Accreditation Council of Graduate Medical Education
American Association of Colleges of Osteopathic Medicine
Association of American Medical Colleges
American Academy of Family Physicians
American Board of Medical Specialties
American College of Surgeons
American Dental Association
American Dental Education Association
American Medical Association
American Medical Student
Association American Osteopathic Association
Centers for Medicare & Medicaid Services
Council on Graduate Medical Education[27]
Department of Education
Educational Commission of Foreign Medical Graduates
Health Resources and Services Administration
Medical Group Management Association
Medicare Payment Advisory Commission
National Resident Matching Program
The Society of Thoracic Surgeons

We conducted our work from September 2008 to April 2009 in accordance with all sections of GAO's Quality Assurance Framework that are relevant to our objectives. The framework requires that we plan and perform the engagement to obtain sufficient and appropriate evidence to meet our stated objectives and discuss any limitations in our work. We believe that the information and data obtained, and the analysis conducted, provide a reasonable basis for any findings and conclusions.

ENCLOSURE V

Comments from the Department of Health and Human Services

Note: Page numbers in the draft report may differ from those in this chapter.

DEPARTMENT OF HEALTH & HUMAN SERVICES OFFICE OF THE SECRETARY

Assistant Secretary for Legislation
Washington, DC 20201

APR 23 2009

Kathleen M. King
Director, Health Care
U.S. Government Accountability Office
441 G Street N.W.
Washington, DC 20548

Dear Ms. King:

Enclosed are comments on the U.S. Government Accountability Office's (GAO) report entitled: "Graduate Medical Education: Trends in Training and Student Debt" (GAO-09-438R).

The Department appreciates the opportunity to review this report before its publication.

Sincerely,

Barbara Pisaro Clark

Barbara Pisaro Clark
Acting Assistant Secretary for Legislation

Attachment

GENERAL COMMENTS OF THE DEPARTMENT OF HEALTH AND HUMAN SERVICES (HHS) ON THE U.S. GOVERNMENT ACCOUNTABILITY OFFICE'S DRAFT REPORT: "GRADUATE MEDICAL EDUCATION: TRANDS IN TRAINING AND STUDENT DEBT" (GAO-09-438R)

The U.S. Department of Health and Human Services, including the Health Resources and Services Administration (HRSA) and the Centers for Medicare and Medicaid Services (CMS), has reviewed the GAO's draft report entitled, "Graduate Medical Education: Trends in Training and Student Debt" (GAO-09-438R).

GAO has made reference on Page 4 (second paragraph, 5th sentence) and on page 17 (first bullet on slide and in the accompanying chart) that there has been an increase in the choice of Family Medicine by United States Medical School Graduates (USMGs). While it is true that the percentage of Family Medicine residency slots filled by USMGs has increased from 2005 to 2009, this is the result of two factors. The first is the number of residency slots offered has decreased by 8 percent, and the second is the number of USMGs filling those slots has decreased by only 4 percent. Moreover, USMGs entering Family Medicine residencies have decreased as a percentage of all USMGs between 2005 and 2009 from 8.1 percent to 7.4 percent. Therefore, HRSA believes stating an increase in the choice of USMGs is misleading and that all references to an increase in Family Practice residencies should be removed from the draft correspondence.

HRSA also suggests that the GAO should include "service obligation" as an additional factor that influences not only the choice of specialty, but where the clinician chooses to practice and for how long. For example, in the article, "Factors Influencing Primary Care Physician's Choice to Practice in Medically Underserved Areas," (Academic Medicine, Vol. 72, No. 10/October Supplement 1, 1997, pages S109 – S111) it was found that these factors strongly influenced the decision to practice in an underserved area. HRSA's National Health Service Corps Scholarship Program requires a scholarship recipient to complete a primary care residency, and the program actively seeks out scholarship recipients with the characteristics which experience has shown are more likely to result in the recipients wanting to practice in underserved areas and remain after fulfillment of the service obligation.

Finally, CMS notes that the draft report does not specifically mention residents training in podiatric programs. Under Medicare, podiatric residents are treated the same way as dental residents.

End Notes

[1] These payments include direct and indirect Medicare graduate medical education payments. Direct payments are provided to teaching institutions for costs directly related to medical training, such as teachers' salaries and administrative costs, while indirect payments are provided for the increased patient care costs associated with medical training. For fiscal year 2008, indirect payments were about 71 percent of total Medicare graduate medical education payments. In addition, Medicare graduate medical payments also subsidize podiatric and dental training.

[2] In part to constrain costs, Congress limited the number of postgraduate medical training positions supported by Medicare with the 1997 Balanced Budget Act. Medicare support for podiatric and dental training positions was not affected by this legislation.

[3] According to the Congressional Research Service, federal and state Medicaid payments for graduate medical education were estimated to be about $3.2 billion in 2005. This estimate was based on 2005 survey data. There is no formal federal reporting mechanism to document Medicaid graduate medical education payments by state.

[4] Medical students received over $1.8 billion in federal guaranteed or direct student loans during the 2006-2007 school year, according to a survey of financial aid offices conducted by the Association of American Medical Colleges.

[5] Program spending totaled about $183 million in fiscal year 2007. This number excludes funding for HRSA student loans, which utilize revolving loan funds derived generally from premium charges, and includes programs for health professionals other than medical school students and graduates, such as physician assistants and dentists.

[6] Department of Veterans Affairs' spending towards medical education in its facilities totaled about $800 million in fiscal year 2008.

[7] The NRMP is affiliated with the Association of American Medical Colleges.

[8] In addition to a matching service for residency programs, the NRMP also administers a matching service for fellowship programs.

[9] Our review of postgraduate medical training trends focused on allopathic residency. Allopathic medicine is a system of medicine that aims to combat disease by using remedies such as drugs or surgery which produce effects that are different from or incompatible with those of the disease being treated; graduates of allopathic medical schools receive a Doctor of Medicine (MD) degree. In contrast, osteopathic medicine is a form of medical practice similar to allopathic medicine that also incorporates manual manipulation of the body as therapy; graduates of osteopathic medical schools receive a Doctor of Osteopathic Medicine (DO) degree. We excluded osteopathic residency because osteopathic residency positions make up less than 6 percent of all residency positions offered by the NRMP and the American Osteopathic Association, the organization that administers the matching service for osteopathic residency. However, osteopathic physicians are included in our review because over 35 percent of osteopathic physicians enter 1st year allopathic postgraduate medical training.

[10] Our review of factors influencing specialty choice focused on medical students enrolled in U.S. medical schools leading to an MD degree. Our literature review found only limited information on the factors that influence osteopathic and international medical school students' specialty choice and interviews we conducted with osteopathic and international medical student groups suggested that factors influencing these students may be similar to those influencing allopathic students.

[11] On-call hours refer to hours when a physician can be contacted outside of regularly scheduled work hours, such as for an emergency.

[12] These loans may be made by private lenders and guaranteed by the federal government or made directly by the federal government through a student's school.

[13] HHS also noted that service obligation influences where physicians practice and the period for which they remain in their practice location. We acknowledge that specialty choice, service obligation, practice location, and duration of practice in a specific location can be interrelated, but for the purposes of this chapter, the issue of physician practice location and its duration were outside our scope.

[14] The NHSC Scholarship Program pays for up to 4 years of support, including tuition, a monthly stipend, and other costs.

[15] Oral and maxillofacial surgery programs last 4 to 6 years.

[16] There is wide variation in the stipends provided to dentists in postgraduate training. Some postgraduate training programs do not provide dentists with stipends, while some may offer dentists over $47,000 annually, according to the American Dental Association (ADA).

[17] Stents are small, permanent tubes placed in arteries to improve blood flow, keep arteries from narrowing or weakening, and prevent blockages.

[18] Allopathic medicine is a system of medicine that aims to combat disease by using remedies such as drugs or surgery which produce effects that are different from or incompatible with those of the disease being treated; graduates of allopathic medical schools receive an MD degree. In contrast, osteopathic medicine is a form of medical practice similar to allopathic

medicine that also incorporates manual manipulation of the body as therapy; graduates of osteopathic medical schools receive a doctor of osteopathic medicine (DO) degree.

[19] We excluded osteopathic residency because osteopathic residency positions make up less than 6 percent of all residency positions offered by the National Resident Matching Program (NRMP) and the American Osteopathic Association, the organization that administers the matching service for osteopathic residency. In addition, we found only limited information on the factors that influence osteopathic and international medical school students' specialty choice and interviews we conducted with osteopathic and international medical student groups suggested that factors influencing these students' decisions may be similar to those influencing allopathic students.

[20] The NRMP is affiliated with the Association of American Medical Colleges (AAMC).

[21] For example, medical students can graduate from (1) a U.S. medical school leading to an MD degree, (2) a U.S. medical school leading to a DO degree, and (3) an international medical school.

[22] U.S. MD students do not have to enter the NRMP match if they enter the military or Canadian matches. According to 2007 data, most physicians in U.S. postgraduate medical training earned an MD degree from a U.S. medical school.

[23] There is some variation as to what specialties are included under primary care. While family medicine, general internal medicine, and general pediatrics are generally accepted as primary care specialties, other specialties that may also be considered primary care include obstetrics/gynecology, psychiatry, preventative medicine, geriatric medicine, and osteopathic general practice.

[24] The GQ survey response rate declined in 2005 when the survey became optional but has since increased.

[25] These data are not verified by the Department of Education (Education); therefore; they may be under or overstated.

[26] Education's repayment plan calculator is available at: http://www.ed.gov/offices/OSFAP/DirectLoan/RepayCalc/dlentry1.html.

[27] We attended its fall 2008 meeting, reviewed presentation materials, and discussed the nature of the council with HRSA, the federal agency that provides support to the council.

In: Cost and Access Issues in Law and Medical... ISBN: 978-1-61122-529-7
Editors: Danielle B. Vesser

Chapter 2

HIGHER EDUCATION: ISSUES RELATED TO LAW SCHOOL COST AND ACCESS

United States Government Accountability Office

October 26, 2009

The Honorable Tom Harkin
Chairman
The Honorable Michael B. Enzi
Ranking Member
Committee on Health, Education, Labor, and Pensions
United States Senate

The Honorable George Miller
Chairman
The Honorable John P. Kline
Ranking Member Committee on Education and Labor
House of Representatives

In order to participate in federal student financial aid programs, law schools must be accredited by an agency recognized by the Department of Education (Education).[1] Accreditation is intended to ensure that schools provide basic levels of quality in their educational programs, and Education recognizes those accrediting agencies that it concludes can reliably determine the quality of education provided by the schools and programs they accredit. The American Bar Association's (ABA) Council of the Section of Legal Education and Admissions to the Bar serves as the main accrediting agency for law schools, and students who attend one of the 200 ABA-accredited law schools can take the bar examination in any jurisdiction in the country. There are also several law schools that are accredited by other Education-recognized accrediting agencies such as the Western Association of Schools and Colleges. Graduates of some of these non-ABA-accredited law schools are eligible to take the bar examination in their own state, but may not do so nationwide.

The ABA's accreditation standards focus on a number of issues, including schools' facilities, student support services, faculty, admissions practices, and graduates' passage of the bar exam. Concerns have been raised about how some of these accreditation standards may affect the cost of attendance and minority access. In 2007, we reported on the ABA's process for accrediting law schools and questions that had been raised about the process.[2] In this chapter, in response to a mandate in the Higher Education Opportunity Act,[3] we examine the following questions: (1) How do law schools compare with similar professional schools in terms of cost and minority enrollment? (2) What factors, including accreditation, may affect the cost of law school? (3) What factors, including accreditation, may affect minority access to law school?

We briefed your staff on the results of our analysis on September 2 and 3, 2009, and this chapter formally conveys the information provided during that briefing (see appendix I for the briefing slides). In summary, we reported the following:

- Since 1994, tuition and fees at law schools and selected professional schools have increased, and trends in minority enrollment have been comparable across types of schools. At law, medical, and dental schools during this time period, Hispanics and Asians/Pacific Islanders increased as a share of enrollment or stayed at about the same level, while African American enrollment declined or stayed at about the same level.
- According to law school officials, the move to a more hands-on, resource-intensive approach to legal education and competition among schools for higher rankings appear to be the main factors driving the cost of law school, while ABA accreditation requirements appear to play a minor role. Additionally, officials at public law

schools reported that recent decreases in state funding are a contributor to rising tuition at public schools.

- Most law school officials do not cite ABA accreditation standards as having an impact on minority access at their schools. Lower average Law School Admission Test (LSAT) scores and undergraduate grade point averages (GPA) may have negatively affected some African Americans and Hispanics.

We used the following methodologies to develop our findings. To compare law schools with similar professional schools in terms of cost and minority enrollment, we selected medical, dental, and veterinary schools based on Education's list of first-professional degree programs and the availability of cost and enrollment data, and analyzed data on tuition and enrollment from Education's Integrated Postsecondary Education Data System (IPEDS) for these schools. We determined that IPEDS data are sufficiently reliable for the purposes of this chapter by testing them for accuracy and completeness, reviewing documentation about systems used to produce the data, and interviewing agency officials. Additionally, we analyzed data from the ABA and the Association of American Medical Colleges (AAMC) on students' law and medical school debt. To determine the reliability of these data, we interviewed ABA and AAMC officials about limitations with the data collected and uses of the data. We found these data to be sufficiently reliable for our purposes. We adjusted the historical tuition, fee, and debt data for inflation using the gross domestic product price index.

To examine what factors, including accreditation, may affect law school cost and minority access, we reviewed documentation from the ABA and the Law School Admission Council (LSAC), and analyzed LSAC's data on law school acceptance rates. We also interviewed officials from 22 law schools, including 19 ABA-accredited schools and 3 schools accredited by other agencies recognized by Education (non-ABA-accredited). We selected this nonprobability sample to reflect a range of characteristics, including institutional control (public, private not-for-profit, private for-profit), geographic location, school size, minority enrollment, and average LSAT score (see table 1). Finally, we spoke with a diverse group of law students from 1 ABA-accredited and 1 non-ABA-accredited school, student representatives from 2 minority law student associations, and officials from the ABA and LSAC.

Table 1. Summary of Law School Contacts

Type of law school	Total number of law schools	Sample size
ABA-accredited	200	19
Public	81	9
Private, not-for-profit	113	9
Private, for-profit	6	1
Non-ABA-accredited	11	3
Public	1	0
Private, not-for-profit	7	2
Private, for-profit	3	1
Total	211	22

Source: GAO analysis of Education and ABA data.

We conducted this performance audit from March through August 2009 in accordance with generally accepted government auditing standards. Those standards require that we plan and perform the audit to obtain sufficient, appropriate evidence to provide a reasonable basis for our findings and conclusions based on our audit objectives. We believe that the evidence obtained provides a reasonable basis for our findings and conclusions based on our audit objectives.

We provided copies of a draft of this chapter to the Department of Education and the American Bar Association for review and comment. The Association of American Medical Colleges and the Law School Admission Council received selected excerpts of the report to review the findings related to the respective data they provided, and we made changes as appropriate. Education had no comments on the draft report. The ABA said that the report was generally accurate, balanced, and fair. See appendix II for the ABA's comments.

We are sending copies of this chapter to relevant congressional committees, the Secretary of Education, and other interested parties and will make copies available to others upon request. In addition, this chapter will be available at no charge on GAO's Web site at www.gao.gov.

If you or your staff has any questions about this chapter, please contact me at (202) 512-7215 or scottg@gao.gov. Contact points for our Offices of Congressional Relations and Public Affairs may be found on the last page of this chapter. GAO staff members who made key contributions to this chapter are listed in appendix III.

George A. Scott
Director, Education, Workforce,
and Income Security Issues

APPENDIX I: BRIEFING SLIDES

Higher Education: Issues Related to Law School Cost and Access

Briefings for the Senate Committee on Health, Education, Labor, and Pensions and the House Committee on Education and Labor

September 2009

Overview

- Research Objectives
- Scope and Methodology
- Summary of Findings
- Background
- Findings

Research Objectives

In response to a mandate in the Higher Education Opportunity Act,[4] we addressed the following questions:

1. How do law schools compare with similar professional schools in terms of cost and minority enrollment?
2. What factors, including accreditation requirements, may affect the cost of law school?
3. What factors, including accreditation requirements, may affect minority access to law school?

Scope and Methodology

To address our research objectives, we:

- Reviewed documentation from the American Bar Association (ABA) and the Law School Admission Council (LSAC).
- Identified medical, dental, and veterinary schools as the most appropriate similar professional schools based on the Department of Education's (Education) list of first-professional degree programs and the availability of cost and enrollment data on these schools.
- Analyzed data on tuition and enrollment from Education, the ABA,LSAC, and the Association of American Medical Colleges, and found these data to be sufficiently reliable for our purposes.
    - Data from Education's Integrated Postsecondary Education Data System (IPEDS) covered the period from 1994/1995 through 2007/2008.
    - Data on acceptance rates reflected the period from 2000/2001 though 2007/2008.
    - Data on student debt covered 2001/2002 through 2007/2008.

We interviewed:

- Officials from 22 law schools, including 19 ABA-accredited schools and 3 schools accredited by other agencies recognized by the Department of Education (non-ABA-accredited).
    - We selected this nonprobability sample to reflect a range of institutional control (public, private not-for-profit, private for-profit), geographic location, school size, minority enrollment, and average Law School Admission Test (LSAT) score.
- A diverse group of law students from one ABA-accredited and one non-ABA-accredited school.
- Representatives of two minority law student associations, the ABA, and other professional associations.
- We conducted this performance audit from March to August 2009, in accordance with generally accepted government auditing standards.
- Those standards require that we plan and perform the audit to obtain sufficient, appropriate evidence to provide a reasonable basis for our findings and conclusions based on our audit objectives.

- We believe that the evidence obtained provides a reasonable basis for our findings and conclusions based on our audit objectives.

Summary of Findings

Multiple Factors May Affect Law School Cost and Access; Accreditation Requirements Do Not Appear to Be a Major Driver

- Since 1994, tuition and fees at law schools and selected professional schools have increased, and trends in minority enrollment have been comparable across types of schools. At law, medical, and dental schools during this time period, Hispanics and Asians/Pacific Islanders increased as a share of enrollment or stayed at about the same level, while African American enrollment declined or stayed at about the same level.
- According to law school officials, the move to a more hands-on, resource-intensive approach to legal education and competition among schools for higher rankings appear to be the main factors driving law school cost, while ABA accreditation requirements appear to play a minor role. Additionally, recent decreases in state funding are seen as a contributor to rising tuition at public schools.
- Most law school officials do not cite ABA accreditation standards as having an impact on minority access at their schools. Lower average LSAT scores and undergraduate grade point averages (GPA) may have negatively affected some African Americans and Hispanics.

Background

Law School Accreditation

- To be eligible to participate in federal student aid programs, a postsecondary school must be accredited by an agency recognized by the Department of Education.[5]
    - The ABA's Council of the Section of Legal Education and Admissions to the Bar is recognized for accrediting law schools.

- Some law schools that are not accredited by the ABA have obtained accreditation from other agencies that are recognized by the Department of Education.
- Graduate and professional students at these schools may be eligible to borrow up to $20,500 per year in federal Stafford loans, as well as additional Graduate/Professional PLUS loans.

Background

ABA Accreditation Requirements

- The ABA's *Standards and Rules of Procedure for Approval of Law Schools* establish requirements with which law schools must comply to be accredited by the ABA.
- Standards focus on issues such as curriculum, student support, faculty, and admissions.
- As of June 2008, 200 law schools had received ABA accreditation.
    - Nine of the 200 were provisionally accredited.
    - Since 1952, only 8 institutions have applied for but never received accreditation.

A J.D. Degree from an ABA-Accredited Law School Provides Eligibility to Take the Bar Exam in Any U.S. Jurisdiction, and for Some States It Is a Prerequisite

Educational Pipeline: African Americans and Hispanics Have Lower Educational Attainment than Whites and Asians/Pacific Islanders, Reducing the Pool of Potential Law School Applicants

Educational Attainment for 25-to 40-Year-Olds in 2007

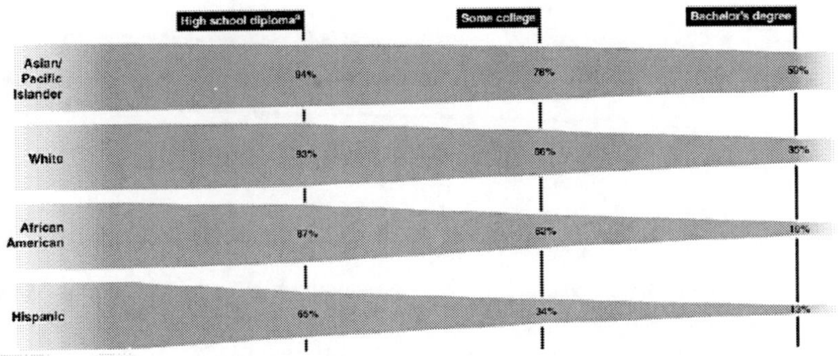

Source: GAO analysis of 2007 American Community Survey data.

Note: Unlike other data sources used in this chapter, the American Community Survey collects data on a sample of the population. All differences in levels of educational attainment between racial/ethnic groups are statistically significant. [a]Highschool diploma includes equivalent qualifications, such as the GED.

Finding 1: Comparing Professional Schools—Cost

Tuition and Fees at Law and Other Professional Schools Have Increased since 1994

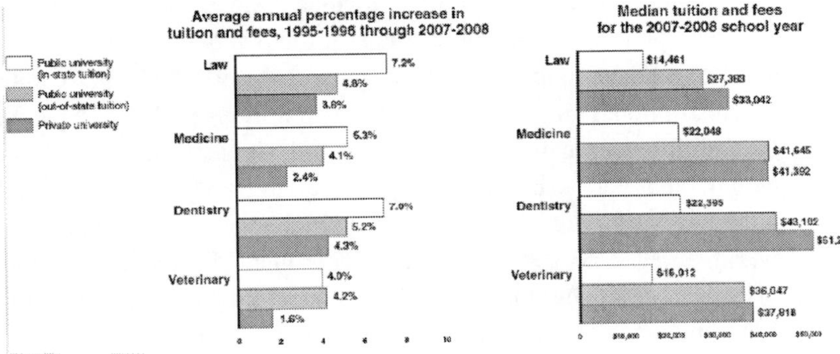

Source: GAO analysis of Education's IPEDS data.

Note: All figures have been adjusted to 2009 dollars.

Average Professional School Debt for Law and Medical School Graduates Has Risen since 2001

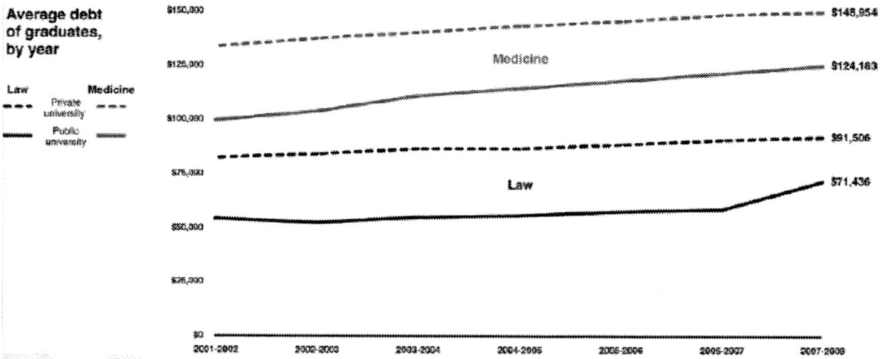

Source: GAO analysis of American Bar Association and Associationof American Medical Colleges data.

Note: All figures have been adjusted to 2007 dollars. Data on average professional school debt were not available for the other professional programs we examined. Data were not available prior to 2001.

Grants and Scholarships Can Lower the Net Cost of Tuition and Fees for Some Students

- All professional degree programs we examined offer institutional aid–such as grants, scholarships, tuition remission, and loan repayment assistance–that can lower the cost of attendance for students who receive it. For example according to ABA data, in 2006-2007:
  - Public law schools provided an average of $3,271 per capita in institutional aid, which offset median resident tuition by about 24 percent and median nonresident tuition by about 12 percent.
  - Private law schools provided an average of $7,542 per capita in institutional aid, which offset median tuition by about 24 percent.
- In addition to receiving institutional aid, students at law, medical, dental, and veterinary schools are able to apply for a number of federalgrants and scholarships, such as Scholarships for Disadvantaged Students from the Department of Health and Human Services, and Thurgood Marshall Legal Educational Opportunity Program assistance through the Department of Education.

Finding 1: Comparing Professional Schools—Enrollment

Since 1994-1995, African Americans Have Declined as a Share of Enrollment in Law Programs, while Their Share of Medical and Dental Enrollment Has Fluctuated

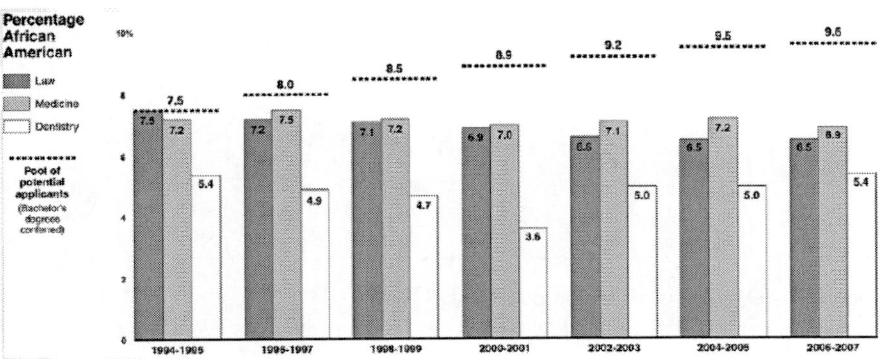

Source: GAO analysis of Education's IPEDS data.

Note: Comparable data on average enrollment by race/ethnicity were not available for veterinary medicine programs. Data are for non-Hispanic African Americans.

Since 1994-1995, Hispanics Have Increased as a Share of Enrollment in Law and Dental Programs, while Their Share of Medical Enrollment Has Fluctuated

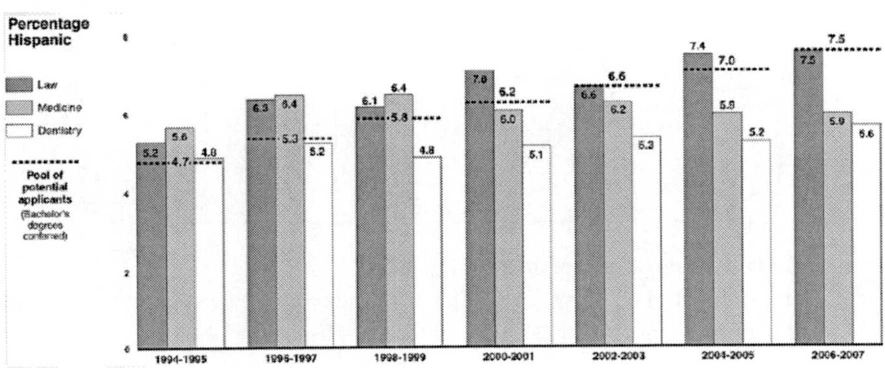

Source: GAO analysis of Education's IPEDS data.

Note: Comparable data on average enrollment by race/ethnicity were not available for veterinary medicine programs.

Since 1994-1995, Asians/Pacific Islanders Have Increased as a Share of Enrollment in Law and Medical Programs, while Their Share of Dental Enrollment Has Fluctuated

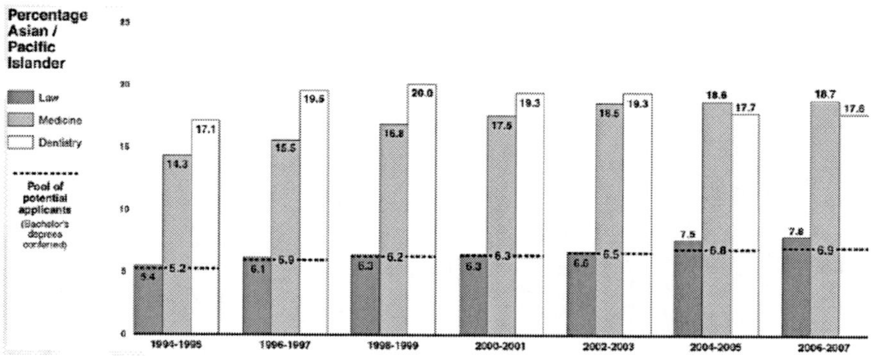

Source: GAO analysis of Education's IPEDS data.

Note: Comparable data on average enrollment by race/ethnicity were not available for veterinary medicine programs.

Since 1994-1995, Whites Have Declined as a Share of Enrollment in Law, Medical, and Dental Programs

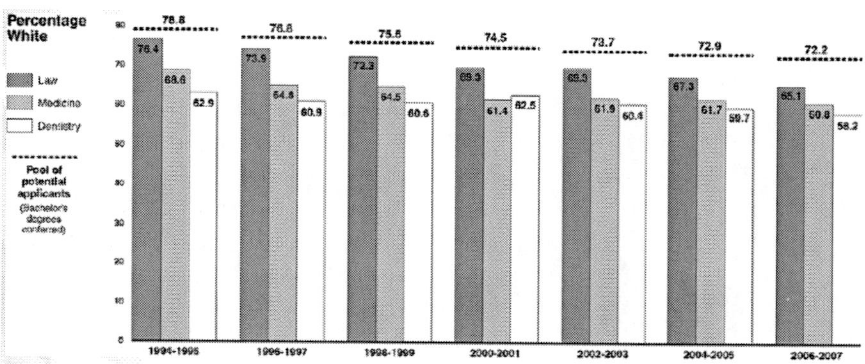

Source: GAO analysis of Education's IPEDS data.

Note: Comparable data on average enrollment by race/ethnicity were not available for veterinary medicine programs. Data are for non-Hispanic whites.

Finding 2: Factors Affecting Cost

The Change to a More Hands-on, Resource-Intensive Approach to Legal Education and Competition among Schools for Higher Rankings Reportedly Have Affected Cost

- Officials from most ABA-accredited schools we interviewed reported that changes in the approach to legal education have affected cost, particularly in the areas of faculty and staff. These changes include:
  - increased emphasis on hands-on clinical experiences, and smaller skills-based courses;
  - increased diversity of course offerings–e.g., international law and environmental law; and
  - increased student support–e.g., academic support, career services, and admissions support.
- Officials at most of the ABA-accredited law schools we spoke with and student representatives reported that schools compete to attract students and faculty and to increase their *U.S. News and World Report* ranking. This competition has had an impact on cost because:
  - Rankings are determined in part by such cost-related factors as per student expenditures, student-faculty ratio, and library resources.
  - According to law school officials, schools offer clinics and diverse elective courses to compete for students.
  - To attract the best faculty, school officials reported that they may offer higher salaries.

ABA Accreditation Is Reportedly Not a Major Driver of Cost

- Officials from most ABA-accredited schools we spoke with reported that ABA accreditation requirements were not a major driver of cost increases in legal education.
- Officials from more than half of the ABA-accredited schools we spoke with stated they would meet or exceed some ABA accreditation standards even if they were not required. School officials noted that the standards often follow market trends and changing approaches to legal education.

    - For example, according to ABA data, student-faculty ratios are generally lower than the ABA standards require (20:1).
    - Officials from most of the schools we spoke to said they would offer skills-based courses and clinical opportunities (which are required by the ABA standards) in response to shifting expectations about the experiences students will need to be successful in the legal field.
- Officials from a few ABA-accredited schools noted major capital costs that may be required to meet ABA accreditation standards, such as library expansion, may be covered by endowment funds or alumni donations.
- However, accreditation may increase costs for a small number of schools.
    - Officials at one ABA-accredited school reported increasing spending on bar exam preparation support in response to ABA concerns about its bar passage rate.
    - Officials at some ABA-accredited schools said that ABA accreditation standards related to libraries may impose costs because they find the standards do not clearly describe the required size and organization of library collections.
    - Officials at two of the three non-ABA accredited law schools stated they would have to spend significant resources to become ABA-accredited.[6]
- In some instances, accreditation standards may limit experimentation with potentially lower-cost approaches. For example, officials at some of the ABA-accredited and all of the non-ABA-accredited schools we contacted said the standards could affect schools that wanted to take steps such as:
    - expanding the role of non-tenure track and adjunct faculty,
    - developing predominantly electronic libraries, and
    - delivering courses online.

Officials at Public Law Schools Report That Decreased State Funding Has Contributed to Increased Tuition and Fees

- Most public law school officials we spoke with emphasized recent decreases in state funding as a contributor to rising tuition.

- The tuition and fees at some public schools rival those of selective private institutions. For example, in 2008, six public law schools had resident tuition and fees greater than $30,000.
- A limited number of public law schools have maintained relatively low prices, but their tuition is increasing:
    - In 2008, public law schools in the South had the lowest tuition and fees, for both residents and nonresidents, while tuition was highest in the Northeast.
    - The average annual percentage increase in tuition was highest in the West and in the South.

Finding 3: Minority Access to Law School

Acceptance Rates for Each Racial/Ethnic Group Have Followed Similar Patterns since 2000, with African Americans Having the Lowest Rates of Acceptance

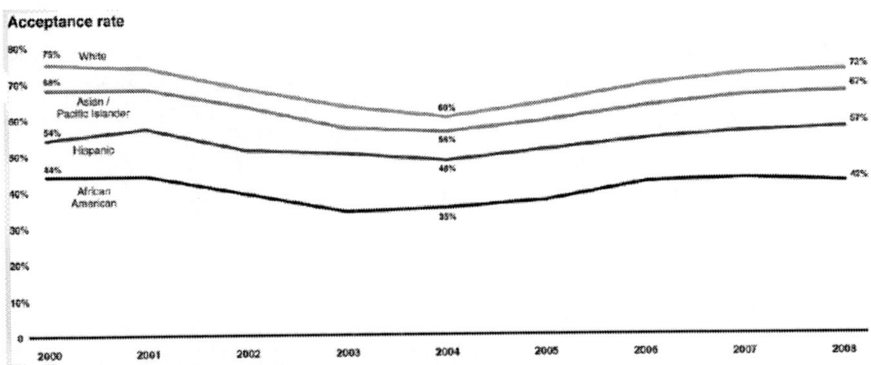

Source: GAO analysis of Law School Admission Council data.

Note: The acceptance rate is the percentage of applicants in each group who were accepted by at least one law school. During the time period shown, the Law School Admission Council allowed applicants to select only one racial/ethnic category.

With a Few Exceptions, Law School Officials Do Not Cite ABA Accreditation Standards as Having an Impact on Minority Access at Their Schools

- Most law school officials, students, and minority student group representatives we interviewed focused on issues such as differences in LSAT scores, academic preparation, and professional contacts, rather than accreditation standards, to explain minority access issues.

- However, officials from some law schools reported that accreditation standards may affect minority access. For example:
    - An official at one ABA-accredited law school said the ABA's standards related to bar passage and admissions make schools less likely to admit applicants with low LSAT scores because they put the schools at risk of not meeting these standards. Officials at a few other ABA-accredited schools said that the bar passage standard did not affect their own admissions policies, but could affect access at less selective schools.
    - Officials at a non-ABA-accredited school reported that seeking ABA accreditation would require them to institute much stricter admissions standards, to the potential disadvantage of minorities with lower average LSAT scores.

A Variety of Elements Contribute to the Strength of an Individual's Application Package

- Officials at nearly all of the schools we spoke with said that they consider a number of elements in an application package, including:
    - LSAT score,
    - Undergraduate GPA,
    - Letters of recommendation, and
    - Personal statement.
- Admission to law school depends, in part, on the strength of the overall package.

Lower Average LSAT Scores and Undergraduate GPAs May Have Negatively Affected Some African Americans and Hispanics

- According to LSAC's analysis, African American and Hispanic law school applicants had lower average LSAT scores and undergraduate GPAs than white and Asian/Pacific Islander applicants.
- LSAC cautions that LSAT scores should not be the only admissions criterion, and that scores are only a partial predictor of first-year law school performance.

- Some law school officials said that schools compete for minority applicants with above-average LSAT scores.
- However, according to representatives from LSAC, the ABA, some law schools, and one minority student group, schools are reluctant to admit applicants with lower LSAT scores because the median LSAT score is a key factor in the *U.S. News and World Report* rankings.
- Officials from a few schools noted that their reluctance to admit applicants with lower undergraduate GPAs stems from a concern that these students would be less able to compete academically in law school.

Various Factors May Influence Differences in LSAT Scores among Racial/Ethnic Groups

- Officials from law schools and LSAC and law students suggested a number of reasons for the LSAT score gap:
  - Differences in academic preparation throughout the educational pipeline.
  - Resources for preparation: African American and Hispanic students, a higher proportion of whom come from low-income backgrounds compared with whites, may be less able to afford to take LSAT prep courses or time off to study for the LSAT.
  - The broader pattern of racial/ethnic differences in standardized test scores.

    The Higher Education Opportunity Act required Education to enterinto an agreement with the National Academy of Sciences to conduct a study to identify any race, ethnicity, or gender bias in the content and construction of standardized tests used for admission to institutions of higher education.[7] An interim report is due from the academy in August 2010.

African American and Hispanic Applicants May Have Fewer Prof-essional Contacts to Draw Upon in the Application Process

- Officials from two ABA-accredited law schools and some law students said that African American and Hispanic law school applicants may be disadvantaged because:

- Fewer applicants in these groups may have contact with lawyers or other professionals who could advise them on aspects of the application process, such as how to prepare for the LSAT.
- These applicants may have fewer contacts to write letters of recommendation.

Law School Cost May Affect Minority Students, but It Is Unclear How Cost Influences Students' Decisions to Apply to and Enroll in Law School

- Some law school officials we interviewed stated that rising law school tuition may have disproportionately affected minority students, a large proportion of whom are low income.
- Officials from two ABA-accredited schools and one minority law student association we interviewed said that some minority students may have faced challenges securing private or federal Graduate/Professional PLUS loans because of poor credit or the lack of a cosigner.
- Cost is one of a number of factors that may affect the decision to apply to and enroll in law school. Because data are not readily available on how potential applicants make these decisions, the impact of cost on minority access is unclear.

The Percentage of Law Schools Whose Tuition Can Be Fully Funded through Lower-Interest Stafford Loans Has Decreased over Time

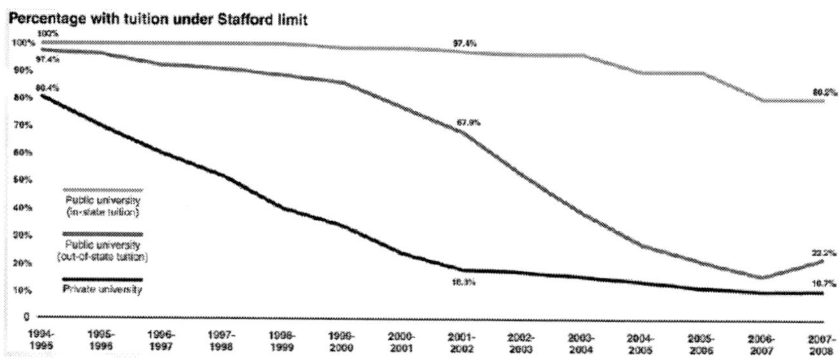

Source: GAO analysis of Education's IPEDS data

Note: The total Stafford loan limit for graduate students was $18,500 from 1994-1995 through 2006-2007, and $20,500 in 2007-2008.

Law School Officials Reported Various Efforts to Improve Diversity

- At some of the schools we contacted, officials said that they actively recruit minority students, for example, by visiting universities with high percentages of minorities and participating in summer institutes to help minority students prepare for law school.
- A few of the schools we contacted are involved in initiatives tohelp address the pipeline issue, such as mentoring programs for minority or low-income high school students.
- Nearly all the schools we contacted have a variety of support services for students once they enroll, such as academic support programs and career counseling. Officials at a few schools said that these services had expanded in recent years.
- Officials from some public institutions reported that their efforts to increase minority access are constrained by legal restrictions against considering race in admissions.

APPENDIX II: COMMENTS FROM THE AMERICAN BAR ASSOCIATION

Defending Liberty
Pursuing Justice

AMERICAN BAR ASSOCIATION

Section of Legal Education and Admissions to the Bar
Office of the Consultant on Legal Education to the American Bar Association
321 N. Clark Street
Chicago, IL 60654-7598
(312) 988-6738
FAX: (312) 988-5681
E-mail: legaled@abanet.org
http://www.abanet.org/legaled

October 2, 2009

Via Email and
Via UPS Overnight
George A. Scott,
Director
Education, Workforce, and Income Security Issues
General Accountability Office
441 G St., NW, Room 5970
Washington, DC 20548

RE: Draft Report: *Issues Related to Law School Cost and Access (GAO-10-20)*

Dear Mr. Scott:

I am writing to provide comments from the American Bar Association ("ABA") Section on Legal Education and Admissions to the Bar (the "Section") on the draft report, *Issues Related to Law School Cost and Access*. First, let me commend you and your staff on the professionalism with which you conducted the research and produced the report. In our interactions, you were always thoughtful and respectful. As a result of these efforts, the Section believes the draft report is generally accurate, balanced and fair. While we do not necessarily agree with all of the reported comments by respondents, we see no material mistakes or errors in the objective data and information reported. This is a thorough and professional presentation.

The Section staff made every effort to cooperate fully and in a timely fashion with your data requests and to provide other relevant documentation. We believe we responded to your questions and presented information and data to your staff demonstrating that, while there are certain costs associated with accreditation (both direct costs and compliance costs), those costs have been a de minimus factor regarding the growth in the costs of legal education over the last twenty years.

We are pleased to see the conclusion stated on page 2 of Mr. Scott's draft transmittal letter stating that "According to law school officials, the move to a more hands-on, resource intensive approach to legal education and competition among law schools for higher rankings appear to be the main factors driving the cost of law school, while ABA accreditation requirements appear to play a minor role". Your conclusion, based upon the sampling done of law school deans and others, replicates the conclusions reached by the Section in its own study of law school costs conducted in 2002/03.

45621-1 Page 1 10/2/2009

George A. Scott,
Director
Education, Workforce, and Income Security Issues

We were also pleased to see the statement that "Most law school officials do not cite ABA accreditation standards as having an impact on minority access at their schools." We believe that, in the context of the report, this statement refers to the absence of a "negative" impact on diversity efforts by law schools. The ABA Standards, of course, encourage law schools to have a diverse student body, faculty and staff. The data shows substantial growth in diversity of the professorate and the number of deans of ABA-approved law schools over the last eight years (2000-2008) and also shows growth, although relatively slower, in minority enrollment during the same period (20.6 % vs. 21.9%).The findings in the report confirm the Section's conclusions on the diversity issues.

I wish to express the appreciation of the Council and staff of the ABA Section for a carefully and professionally done report. Thank you for the opportunity to respond to it.

Sincerely,

Hulett H. Askew
Consultant on Legal Education

cc: Jerome C. Hafter, Esq.
Honorable Christine M. Durham
Henry F. White, Jr., Executive Director

45621-1 Page 2 10/2/2009

End Notes

[1] 20 U.S.C. § 1099b(j).
[2] GAO, *Higher Education: Issues Related to Law School Accreditation,* GAO-07-314 (Washington, D.C.: Mar. 8, 2007).

[3] Pub. L. No 110-315, sec. 952, § 3001(i), 122 Stat. 3078, 3473 (2008).

[4] Pub. L. No 110-315, sec. 952, § 3001(i), 122 Stat. 3078, 3473 (2008).

[5] 20 U.S.C. § 1099b(j). In 2007, we reported on Education's process for recognizing accrediting agencies and law school accreditation issues. See GAO, *Higher Education: Issues Related to Law School Accreditation,* GAO-07-314 (Washington, D.C.: Mar. 8, 2007).

[6] These schools are accredited by other accrediting bodies recognized by Education.

[7] Pub. L. No. 110-315, § 1110, 122 Stat. 3078, 3496 (2008).

In: Cost and Access Issues in Law and Medical... ISBN: 978-1-61122-529-7
Editors: Danielle B. Vesser

Chapter 3

HIGHER EDUCATION: ISSUES RELATED TO LAW SCHOOL ACCREDITATION

United States Government Accountability Office

ABBREVIATIONS

ABA	American Bar Association Education Department of Education
NACIQI	National Advisory Committee on Institutional Quality and Integrity

March 8, 2007

The Honorable George Miller
Chairman
The Honorable Howard P. "Buck" McKeon
Ranking Minority Member
Committee on Education and Labor
House of Representatives

The Honorable Stephanie Tubbs Jones
House of Representatives

In order to participate in certain federal programs, such as federal student financial aid, postsecondary institutions must be accredited by an accrediting agency recognized by the Department of Education (Education). Accreditation ensures that schools provide basic levels of quality in their educational programs, and Education recognizes those agencies it concludes can reliably determine the quality of education provided by the schools and programs they accredit. Since 1952, Education has recognized the American Bar Association (ABA) as an accrediting agency for law schools. ABA accreditation is important to the 195 law schools it accredits because it allows their graduates the flexibility to take the Bar exam in any jurisdiction in the United States.

The Department of Education requires that all recognized accrediting agencies periodically reapply for continued recognition. The Secretary of Education's accreditation advisory group, the National Advisory Committee on Institutional Quality and Integrity (NACIQI), considered the ABA's most recent application for continued recognition in December 2006. The ABA was originally scheduled for review in December 2005, but Education postponed it twice based on the large volume of public comments that had to be reviewed, as well as concerns about the ABA's diversity standard. To address your interest in these issues, we answered the following questions: (1) What is Education's process for recognizing accrediting agencies? (2) What is ABA's process for accrediting law schools? (3) What concerns have been raised about the ABA's accreditation process?

We used the following methodologies to develop our findings. To understand Education and ABA processes related to accreditation, we reviewed relevant laws and regulations, ABA accreditation standards, and documents pertaining to the ABA's application for renewed recognition. We also interviewed Education officials, ABA representatives, and four law school administrators. To identify the concerns that have been raised about ABA's accreditation process, we reviewed third-party comments submitted to Education in advance of the NACIQI meeting. We also attended the December 2006 public meeting that NACIQI held to consider ABA's application for continued recognition, and reviewed the transcript of the meeting. Finally, we analyzed ABA data on first-year law school enrollment and found the data sufficiently reliable for our purposes. We conducted our work between October 2006 and February 2007 in accordance with generally accepted government auditing standards.

We briefed your staff on results of our analysis on February 9, 2007. This chapter formally conveys the information provided during that briefing. In summary, we reported the following findings:

- Education has established criteria for recognizing an accrediting agency and has mechanisms in place to assess compliance with the criteria. Agencies found to be in compliance with Education's criteria can be approved for up to 5 years. There are also mechanisms in place to defer or deny an agency's recognition.
- ABA has established standards for approval of law schools and has mechanisms in place to assess compliance with the criteria. Law schools are eligible for provisional approval when they demonstrate that they are in substantial compliance with each of the standards, and must demonstrate they are in full compliance to be fully approved.
- Some Education staff, law school administrators, and other third-parties have raised concerns about ABA's accreditation process, particularly with respect to the transparency and consistency of the process, as well as the legality of its diversity standard, which requires schools to demonstrate they are reaching out to underrepresented groups. Based on concerns that ABA is not fully in compliance with regulatory provisions that govern accreditation, Education and NACIQI have recommended that the Secretary of Education renew ABA's recognition for a period of 18 months, rather than the maximum period of 5 years.

We provided copies of a draft of this chapter to the Department of Education and the American Bar Association for review and comment. In written comments, Education provided technical comments and clarifications, which we incorporated as appropriate. In particular, Education clarified that its recommendation suggested that NACIQI require ABA to submit interim reports on ABA's compliance with all criteria for accreditation recognition, not just the diversity standard as stated in the draft. We revised our report accordingly. However, we note that the recommended interim reporting requirements focus heavily on the diversity standard. Education also expressed concern about our characterization of why NACIQI excluded from its recommendation the additional reporting requirements related to diversity, as Education had recommended. Our report correctly notes that NACIQI did not think additional reporting related to the diversity standard was necessary because Education had not identified any instances in which ABA inconsistently applied the diversity standard or provided evidence that law schools had been compelled to violate existing state laws. However, Education thought our report should also note that NACIQI did not address Education's broader concern that ABA had not demonstrated that it has effective controls in place to prevent inconsistent application of the standard as required by the recognition criteria. While Education is correct that NACIQI did not discuss this concern specifically, it addressed these concerns by affirming Education's recommendation to limit ABA's recognition to a period of 18 months. Education's comments appear in appendix II.

The ABA said that the report was generally balanced and fair, and provided technical comments and clarifications, which we incorporated as appropriate. ABA expressed concern about our statement that it uses thresholds on bar passage and attrition rates to prompt further review. ABA emphasized that these thresholds are not used to determine whether or not a school is in compliance with the accreditation standards. We revised our report to clarify this issue. The ABA also provided updated data on law school enrollment that was not available to us at the time we conducted our briefing. Finally, with respect to the background information the report provides on non-ABA approved law schools, the ABA said the number of such law schools is much greater than indicated in our draft report. Specifically, ABA identified a number of California law schools that were not included on the list of non-ABA approved law schools that we obtained from the Law School Admission Council (LSAC). While the information from LSAC is not exhaustive, it provides the most complete source of readily-available data on non-ABA approved law schools. Additionally, because graduates of these law schools can sit for the bar exam in California, our overall message remains the same--graduates of many non-ABA law schools can take the bar exam in the state where they earned their degree. ABA's comments appear in appendix III.

We are sending copies of this chapter to relevant congressional committees, the Secretary of Education, and other interested parties and will make copies available to others upon request. In addition, this chapter will be available at no charge on GAO's Web site at www.gao.gov.

If you or your staff has any questions about this chapter, please contact me at (202) 512-7215 or scottg@gao.gov. Contact points for our Offices of Congressional Relations and Public Affairs may be found on the last page of this chapter. Key contributors to this chapter include Jeff Appel (Assistant Director), Debra Prescott (Analyst-in-Charge), Summer Pachman, John Mingus, and Jim Rebbe.

George A. Scott
Acting Director, Education, Workforce, and Income Security Issues

APPENDIX I: BRIEFING SLIDES

Issues Related to Law School Accreditation

Briefing for the House Committee on Education and Labor and Representative Stephanie Tubbs Jones

February 9, 2007

Briefing Overview

- Introduction
- Research Objectives
- Scope and Methodology
- Background
- Research Findings
- Next Steps in the Recognition Process

Introduction

- Concerns have been raised about trends in law school enrollment for certain racial/ethnic groups.
- Questions have been raised about the transparency of the American Bar Association's (ABA) accreditation process for law schools.
- Questions have also been raised about the extent to which ABA is consistently applying its standards.

Research Objectives

1. What is Education's process for recognizing accrediting agencies?
2. What is ABA's process for accrediting law schools?
3. What concerns have been raised about ABA's accreditation process?

Scope and Methodology

To address our research objectives, we:

- Reviewed relevant laws, regulations, ABA accreditation standards, and documents related to ABA's request for renewed recognition, including third party comments submitted to Education.
- Interviewed Education officials, ABA representatives, and four law school administrators about the accreditation process.
- Analyzed data from ABA on first-year law school enrollment, and found the data sufficiently reliable for our purposes.
- Conducted the review from October 2006 to February 2007 in accordance with generally accepted government auditing standards.

Background

- To be eligible to participate in certain federal programs, such as federal student aid, a postsecondary school must be accredited by an accrediting agency recognized by the Department of Education.
- Education recognizes agencies that it determines to be reliable authorities in determining the quality of education provided by the schools and programs they accredit.
- The American Bar Association's (ABA) Council of the Section of Legal Education and Admissions to the Bar is recognized for accrediting law schools.

History of ABA as a Recognized Accrediting Agency

- First began approving law schools in 1921, and federally recognized since 1952.
    - Must petition for continued recognition at least every 5 years.
- Most recently reviewed in December 2006 after being postponed twice based on high volume of public comments and concerns about the legality of ABA's standards related to diversity.
- As of January 2007, 195 law schools have received ABA approval.
    - Seven provisionally approved; two on probation.

- Since 1952, only eight institutions have applied for but never received approval.
- According to ABA, it is not uncommon for law schools to apply more than once before being approved.
    - Since 1990, 8 of 22 law schools were denied provisional approval at least once before being approved.

J.D. Degree from ABA-Approved Law School Provides Eligibility to Take Bar Exam in Any U.S. Jurisdiction, and for Some States It Is a Prerequisite

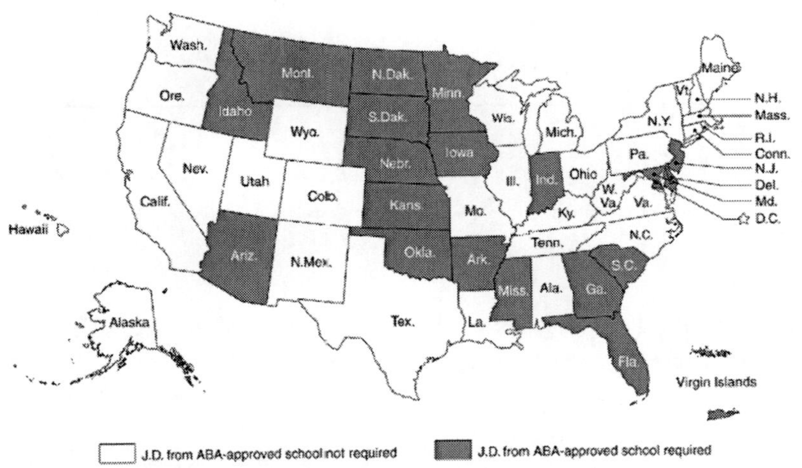

Source: American Bar Association (data); map. Map Resources (presentation).

Graduates from Many Non-ABA approved Law Schools Can Take Bar Exam in Their State

- Of the 41 law schools identified by the Law School Admission Council as non-ABA approved, graduates from 37 can take bar exam in their state.
    - Over half of these schools are in California, which allows graduates of non-ABA approved law schools in the state to take the bar exam.
    - Seven of these schools offer J.D. programs through distance education, but the ABA will not accredit schools that require more than 12 hours of credit via distance.
- Six of the 41 schools are in the process of applying for ABA approval.

- Five of these have not been open long enough to graduate their first class of J.D. students.

Percent First Year Law School Enrollment for Selected Minorities, 1971-2006

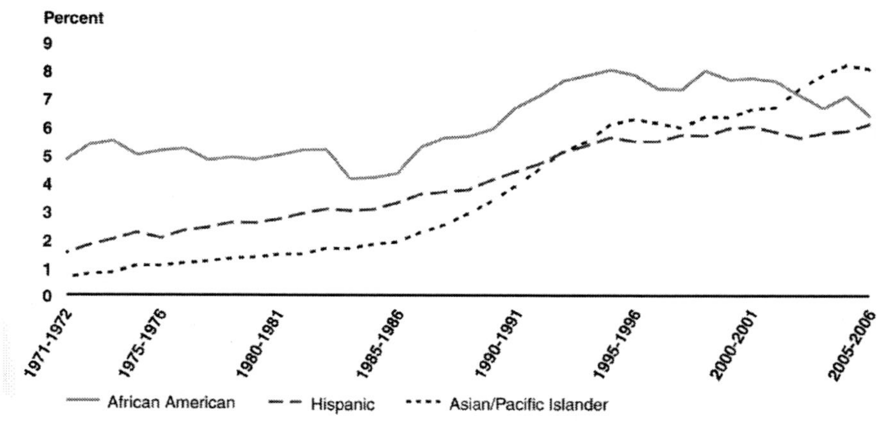

Source: GAO analysis of ABA data.

In Recent Years African American Enrollment has Declined While Asian and Hispanic Enrollment has Increased

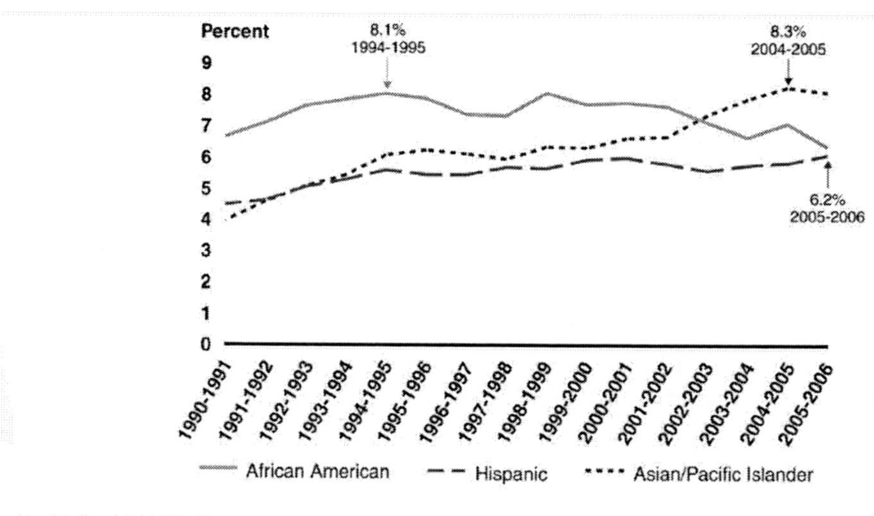

Source: GAO analysis of ABA data.

Objective 1: Education's Process

Education Has Established Criteria for Recognizing an Accrediting Agency

To establish eligibility accreditors must, among other things, demonstrate they:

- Have at least 2 years of accrediting experience.
- Have the capability to administer its accreditation activities.
- Are separate and independent, both administratively and financially, of any related trade association or membership organization if the accreditor is recognized for federal student aid purposes.

Accreditors must have standards for assessing institutional or programmatic quality, and consistently apply and enforce standards.

- Establish standards to assess quality in areas such as student achievement, admissions, curricula, faculty, facilities, support services, fiscal and administrative capacity.
- Establish regular intervals for reevaluating accredited institutions or programs, and processes for approving substantive changes.
- Make final accreditation decisions publicly available.
- Review complaints against itself in timely, fair, and equitable manner.

Education Has Mechanisms in Place to Assess Compliance with Criteria

- Accreditor submits application for recognition.
- Education makes initial recommendation based on review of petition and third-party comments.
- Accreditor invited to respond with additional support, and Education modifies analysis and recommendation, as appropriate.
- Education forwards complete package to the Secretary of Education's accreditation advisory group, the National Advisory Committee on Institutional Quality and Integrity (NACIQI).
- Following public meetings to consider each accrediting agency's petition, NACIQI recommends that the Secretary approve, deny, or defer request.

- Secretary considers entire record of application, including Education staff and NACIQI recommendations, and approves, denies, or defers the request.

Possible Recognition Decision Outcomes

- Approval – Agency recognized for up to 5 years.
- Deferment – deficiencies do not warrant immediate loss of recognition and agency should be able to demonstrate compliance within a maximum of 12 months.
- Denial – If agency fails to comply with criteria or is not effective in its performance.
- Limit, suspend, or terminate recognition of an already recognized agency—can happen anytime.
- Agencies can appeal final decisions.

Objective 2: ABA'S Process

ABA's Organizational Structure for Accreditation Activities

- ABA's accreditation activities fall under the Section of Legal Education and Admissions to the Bar.
- Accreditation and compliance decisions are made by the Section's Council, which is comprised of 21 voting members.
- The Section's Accreditation Committee, which administers the ABA's accreditation process and has primary oversight responsibility for ABA approved law schools, generally makes accreditation recommendations to the Council.
  - The Committee may make accreditation decisions without consulting the Council when schools seeking continued approval are found to be sufficiently in compliance with the standards.
- The Section's Office of the Consultant provides assistance to the Council and the Accreditation Committee.

ABA's Process for Accrediting Law Schools Includes Multiple Levels of Review

- School requesting accreditation completes application, data questionnaire, and self-study and is visited by a site evaluation team.
- Accreditation Committee reviews site evaluation team's report of findings and materials submitted by school and as appropriate, makes final decision or recommendation to Council.
- Council makes final decision to grant, deny, or withdraw accreditation based on Committee's report and all application materials.
  - ABA has requested that the Committee also be recognized by Education as a decision-making body.
  - Due Process – Schools have the right to appeal accreditation decisions.

ABA's Standards for Approval of Law Schools

- ABA considers the extent to which law schools comply with standards in the following areas:
  - Organization and administration
  - Program of legal education
  - Faculty
  - Admissions and student services
  - Library and information resources
  - Facilities
- Provisional approval granted when schools demonstrate substantial compliance with each of the standards; must demonstrate full compliance to be fully approved.

Data Collected on a Range of Indicators

- Data elements collected annually:
  - First-time bar passage
  - Attrition (academic, transfers, etc.)
  - Employment of graduates
  - LSAT scores/Undergraduate GPA
  - Student to faculty ratio

Objective 3: Concerns

Education, School Administrators, and Third-Parties Have Raised Concerns Regarding ABA's Petition for Recognition

- Education, some law school administrators, and others are concerned that ABA has unpublished standards, including minimum LSAT requirements.
    - ABA says it follows its published standards and has no requirement for a minimum LSAT score.
    - ABA acknowledges that indicators such as low bar passage rates and high attrition can prompt further review of other areas, including a school's support services and the credentials of entering students.
        - First-time bar passage rate: < 70 percent overall or more than 10 percentage points below state average.
        - Academic attrition: about 15 to 20 percent.
- Education and other third-parties have expressed concern about ABA's diversity standard, which requires schools to demonstrate a commitment to having both a diverse student body and faculty.
    - Education expressed concern that ABA will evaluate compliance with the standard based in part on the results achieved and that ABA does not have sufficient controls in place to prevent inconsistent application of the standard. Additionally, Education is concerned that the lack of specificity about the requirements would lead the ABA to use unpublished criteria in evaluating compliance.
    - The Chair and Vice Chair of the U.S. Commission on Civil Rights along with other third parties expressed concern that the ABA's diversity standard would put pressure on law schools to employ race conscious admissions and hiring practices, including racial or ethnic quotas.
- The ABA and others defend the current diversity standard:
    - According to ABA representatives, the standard only requires schools to demonstrate that they are reaching out to groups underrepresented in the legal profession. Quotas are not involved and it should not conflict with state laws that prohibit the consideration of race in hiring and admissions.

  - Law school administrators we spoke to and those administrators who provided third-party comments, along with other commenters, were generally supportive of ABA having a diversity standard.
- Education identified instances in which ABA was inconsistently enforcing its standards by allowing some schools to exceed the maximum time allowed to enter compliance without adverse action
  - According to ABA, each instance involved compliance in the areas of bar passage rates or facilities, which cannot be readily addressed in the two-year period schools are given to demonstrate compliance.
  - ABA has approved changes that make clear that if a school has not been able to address noncompliance within the allowable two-year period, ABA must take adverse action or find good cause to extend accreditation.

Next Steps in the Recognition Process for ABA

- Because Education identified a number of compliance issues that ABA could not fully address in advance of the NACIQI meeting, it recommended that NACIQI renew ABA's recognition for a period of 18 months and require the ABA to submit interim reports on its compliance with the criteria for recognition, with particular emphasis on the diversity standard.
  - ABA representatives said they were able to address a number of the concerns immediately, and the remaining items would be addressed by August 2007.
- At a public meeting on 12/4/2006, NACIQI recommended that the Secretary of Education renew ABA's recognition for 18 months; however, it did not recommend any specific reporting requirements related to the diversity standard.
  - NACIQI did not think the reporting requirements related to diversity were necessary given that Education had not identified any instances in which ABA inconsistently applied its diversity standard or provided evidence that law schools had been compelled to violate state laws.
- The ABA is awaiting the final decision from the Secretary of Education on whether its recognition will be renewed.

APPENDIX II: COMMENTS FROM THE DEPARTMENT OF EDUCATION

UNITED STATES DEPARTMENT OF EDUCATION

OFFICE OF POSTSECONDARY EDUCATION

MAR - 1 2007

THE ASSISTANT SECRETARY

Mr. George A. Scott
Acting Director
Education, Workforce, and
Income Security Issues
U.S. Government Accountability Office
441 G Street, NW
Washington, DC 20548

Dear Mr. Scott:

The Department thanks you for the opportunity to comment on the Government Accountability Office's (GAO's) draft report, "HIGHER EDUCATION: Issues Related to Law School Accreditation" (GAO-07-314). Accreditation is an important accountability measure for ensuring the quality of higher education, and we appreciate GAO's study of the Department's significant involvement in this area.

GAO makes no recommendations in this study. In reviewing the content of the draft report, however, the Department has identified the following items that require clarification:

- At page 15 of the Draft Report, in *Objective 1: Education's Process,* GAO has listed three eligibility factors for recognition. Please revise the third bullet to read: "Are separate and independent, both administratively and financially, of any related trade association or membership organization, *if the accreditor is a Title IV, Higher Education Act gatekeeper.*"

- Also on page 15, the fourth bullet should refer to admissions and thus read as follows: "Establish standards to assess quality in areas such as student achievement, *admissions,* curricula, faculty, facilities, support services, fiscal and administrative capacity." The Higher Education Act permits the Department to assess an accrediting agency's standards pertaining to admissions, recruiting, and faculty, 20 U.S.C. § 1099b(a)(5)(C) and (G). The diversity standard of the Council of the Section of Legal Education and Admissions to the Bar of the American Bar Association (ABA) explicitly relates to admissions and faculty hiring. In this vein, the Department staff recommendation found that the ABA's diversity standard (which governs admissions and faculty hiring) fails to comply with 34 C.F.R. §§ 602.18(a) and (b) and 602.23(a)(3), which require effective control mechanisms to ensure consistent accreditation decisions and which bar the use of unpublished accreditation criteria by an accreditation authority.

1990 K STREET, N.W. WASHINGTON, D.C. 20006

Our mission is to ensure equal access to education and to promote educational excellence throughout the Nation.

Page Two – Mr. Scott

- At page 20 of the Draft Report, in its description of the Department staff's concerns about the ABA diversity standard, GAO leaves out an important concern that the Department staff has about the standard—that the agency now intends to evaluate a law school's satisfaction of "its equal opportunity and diversity obligations" based not only on the "totality of actions" (the test under the prior rule) but also on "the results achieved."

- At page 24 of the Draft Report, in the first bullet, GAO leaves the reader with the mistaken impression that the Department staff opposes the use of diversity standards in admissions. The Department staff does not oppose the use of such a standard in admissions but has concerns about requirements specific to the ABA Standard 212. The bullet should thus read as follows: "The ABA and others defend having *Standard 212.*"

- At page 26 of the Draft Report, in the first bullet, GAO erroneously states that the Department recommended that the National Advisory Committee on Institutional Quality and Integrity (NACIQI) require the ABA to submit interim reports only concerning the diversity standard. The Department staff recommendation suggested that NACIQI require interim reports on the ABA's compliance with all criteria for accreditation recognition, not just the diversity standard. The bullet should thus read as follows: "Because Education identified a number of compliance issues that ABA could not fully address in advance of the NACIQI meeting, it recommended that NACIQI renew ABA's recognition for a period of 18 months and require[d] the ABA to submit interim reports *relating to its compliance with the Criteria for Recognition.*"

- The fourth bullet on page 26 of the Draft Report is not entirely accurate. Regarding bar passage rates and Standard 212 (the ABA's diversity standard), the Department staff advised NACIQI that the ABA's lack of effective controls to ensure consistent application of the ABA's standards violated 34 C.F.R. § 602.18(a). §602.18(a) imposes an obligation on the accreditation agency to demonstrate that it "has effective controls against the inconsistent application of the agency's standards." GAO should note that NACIQI did not address this important element of the staff's recommendation.

If you have any questions about these clarifications, please contact Annora Bryant in the Office of the Secretary, Executive Secretariat, at 202-260-1854.

Sincerely,

James F. Manning

James F. Manning
Delegated the Authority of the Assistant Secretary

APPENDIX III: COMMENTS FROM THE AMERICAN BAR ASSOCIATION

ABA Defending Liberty Pursuing Justice

AMERICAN BAR ASSOCIATION

Section of Legal Education and Admissions to the Bar

Office of the Consultant on Legal Education to the American Bar Association
321 N. Clark Street
Chicago, IL 60610-4714
(312) 988-6738
FAX: (312) 988-5681
E-mail: legaled@abanet.org
http://www.abanet.org/legaled

March 1, 2007

George A. Scott
Acting Director
Education, Workforce, and Income Security Issues
General Accountability Office
441 G St., NW
Room 5928
Washington, DC 20548

RE: <u>Draft Report: *Issues Related to Law School Accreditation* (GAO-07-314)</u>

Dear Mr. Scott:

I am writing to provide comments from the American Bar Association's ("ABA") Section on Legal Education and Admissions to the Bar (the "Section") on the draft report, *Issues Related to Law School Accreditation*. First, let me commend Ms. Prescott and your staff on the professionalism with which they conducted their research. In our interactions, they were always pleasant and respectful. As a result of their efforts, the Section believes the draft report is generally balanced and fair; however, there are a few areas that require our response.

<u>Bar Passage</u>

The slide on page 22 of the draft report asserts that "ABA acknowledges that it has unpublished thresholds, and exceeding them can prompt further review." The Section does not use unpublished thresholds in deciding whether a school's bar passage or attrition rates satisfy the Standards for Approval of Law Schools.[1] There are, however, some general characteristics that have, over time, proven to be indicators that further inquiry into a school's bar passage rates might be useful. These characteristics include such things as having a bar passage rate below 60 percent or a weak system of academic support. But, these characteristics alone are not factors for determining compliance or non-compliance with the Standards.

In a December 2005 guidance memorandum, the Section attempted to clarify the factors and process it uses to review a school's bar passage rates. After that memorandum was circulated, a small handful of schools continued to express confusion about whether their bar passage rates complied with the Standards. Thus, the Section

[1] Indeed, the Department itself recently concluded, after a comprehensive review of third-party comments and attendance at a meeting of the Section's Accreditation Committee, that no evidence exists that the Section relies on unwritten standards in its decision-making. *See* Final Determination of Complaints Lodged Against the Council on Legal Education at 8 (Nov. 2, 2006).

George A. Scott
Acting Director

began a process of reviewing and revising its Standards on bar passage in November 2006. The proposed Interpretation of those Standards, which the Council approved to be circulated for comment at its most recent meeting, would require a school to provide additional information demonstrating compliance if its first-time bar passage rates are frequently below 70 percent.

The comment period will conclude in mid-May following an open session to discuss the proposed Interpretation held in conjunction with a meeting of the American Law Institute. After the open session, a final proposed Interpretation, taking into account all of the comments received throughout the comment period, will be issued. The plan is that final consideration by the Council of the proposed Interpretation will occur in June and House of Delegates concurrence will occur in August. If the proposed Interpretation is adopted in its current form, the Section will have a measurable threshold for bar passage rates; however, no such unpublished threshold exists today.

Factors Reviewed if Low Bar Passage Rates Exist

On page 21 of the draft report, GAO indicates that relatively low bar passage rates can prompt a further review of support services and credentials of entering students. This statement is accurate though the list of items that might be reviewed if a school presents low bar passage rates also includes: first-time bar passage rates in other jurisdictions, second-time taker bar passage rates, ultimate bar passage rates, information on academic support, attrition rates, bar preparation programs, and the entering credentials of students.

Diversity

The draft report spends two pages discussing the controversy over the Section's diversity standard. It indicates that in addition to the Department other third parties have expressed concern about the Section's standard. The draft report then describes the comments filed by Gerald Reynolds and Abigail Thernstrom. But, it fails to mention either that their comments were echoed only by four of about 60 third party commenters or that all four of those commenters were special interest groups ideologically opposed to diversity and affirmative action.

Moreover, the draft report's characterization of those who support the Section's diversity standard mentions no specific supporters and only indicates that law school administrators were "generally supportive of ABA having a diversity standard." The real picture is much more stark – no law school dean, judge, or practitioner filed a third-party comment with the Department opposing the Section's standard. And two of the nation's most respected civil rights organizations, the Lawyer's Committee for Civil

George A. Scott
Acting Director

Rights Under Law and the Leadership Conference on Civil Rights, filed comments supporting the Section's standard and explaining the legal basis for its existence. Thus, to accurately reflect the support that exists for the Section's diversity standard, the second bullet on page 24 (slide 21) should provide, "Law school administrators we spoke to and those who provided third-party comments, including the Lawyers Committee for Civil Rights Under Law, the Leadership Conference on Civil Rights, members of the judiciary, and practicing lawyers, were generally supportive of ABA having a diversity standard and contended that the standard did not require the use of quotas or race-conscious admissions programs."

Finally, it is worth noting that the report correctly reflects NACIQI's recommendation to reject any reporting from the Section related to its diversity standard. NACIQI did not believe the Department had identified any instances in which the Section inconsistently applied its diversity standard, nor did it believe that complying with the standard would require schools to violate the law. Thus, as stated in the report, NACIQI disagreed with the Department's contention that the diversity standard would necessarily lead to inconsistent application of the standards and also rejected the Department's recommendation that the Section report on all activities related to the application of its diversity standard.

Minority Enrollments

Page 14 of the draft report contains a chart showing recent figures on minority enrollment in law schools. The chart is accurate but I can provide more recent information which you may wish to add to the chart. On February 15, 2007, the Section distributed to the Deans of all ABA-approved law schools its most recent data on Fall 2006 law school enrollments, including minority enrollments. *See* attached. For the 2006-2007 academic year, there are a total of 9,529 African-American students, (and for information purposes 11,306 Asian students, 2,499 Mexican American students, 551 Puerto Rican students, and 8,564 Other Hispanic students) enrolled in ABA-approved law schools. In other words, 6.8 percent of all enrolled students in an ABA-approved law school in 2006-2007 are African-American, an increase of .6 percent over the 2005-2006 academic year. African-American enrollment in the first-year class is even higher, 7.2 percent, and total minority enrollment for 2006-2007 is 21.6 percent.

Technical Corrections

The draft report asserts on page one that the ABA was "deferred" because of "concerns about the ABA's accreditation process." Later, on page 7, the draft report asserts that the ABA was "deferred" because of concerns about the "ABA's standards related to diversity." It is important to clarify that the Section was not formally deferred by the Department in accordance with the recognition criteria. Instead, the Department administratively postponed its appearance before NACIQI. Also, the April 5, 2006

George A. Scott
Acting Director

letter the Section received from the Department postponing its appearance clearly indicated that the postponement was due to the Department's concern about the Section's standards related to diversity, not because of concerns about the Section's accreditation process. *See* attached letter. Thus, the Section respectfully requests that the draft report be amended to state that the Section was administratively postponed and to state on page one that the April 2006 postponement was due to concerns regarding the Section's diversity standards.

Finally, the draft report on page 12 asserts that there are 41 law schools identified by the Law School Admission Council ("LSAC") as non-ABA approved. Although this statement is true, the number of non-ABA approved law schools in the country is actually much higher. A search of just the non-ABA approved law schools identified by the California Bar Association combined with the LSAC list yields a total of 61 non-ABA approved law schools.

Thank you for providing the Section an opportunity to respond to the draft report. We hope these comments have been helpful and look forward to their incorporation in the final report.

Sincerely,

Hulett H. Askew
Consultant on Legal Education to the
American Bar Association

Cc: Bill Rakes
Hank White
John Przypyszny

Enclosures

42909-1 Page 4

Chapter Sources

The following chapters have been previously published:

Chapter 1 – This is an edited, excerpted and augmented edition of a United States Government Accountability Office publication, Report Order Code GAO-09-438R, dated May 4, 2009.

Chapter 2 – This is an edited, excerpted and augmented edition of a United States Government Accountability Office publication, Report Order Code GAO-10-20, dated October 2009.

Chapter 3 – This is an edited, excerpted and augmented edition of a United States Congressional Research Service publication, Report Order Code GAO-07-314, dated March 2007.

INDEX

M

N

O

P

Q

R

S